Life, Love, and Healing
with
Dissociative Identity Disorder

Pat Suzie Tennent

I AM WE

One Body, Many Parts:
Life, Love, and Healing with
Dissociative Identity Disorder

Pat Suzie Tennent

Pearly Gates Publishing LLC
INSPIRING CHRISTIAN AUTHORS TO BE AUTHORS

Pearly Gates Publishing, LLC, Houston, Texas (USA)

I AM WE -
One Body, Many Parts:
Life, Love, and Healing with Dissociative Identity Disorder

Print ISBN 13: 978-1-947445-83-3
Digital ISBN 13: 978-1-947445-84-0
Library of Congress Control Number: 2020902331

For information and bulk ordering, contact:
Pearly Gates Publishing, LLC
Angela Edwards, CEO
P.O. Box 62287
Houston, TX 77205
BestSeller@PearlyGatesPublishing.com

What Others Are Saying...

Reviews for *Coming Out of the Dark:*
A Memoir of Dissociative Identity Disorder,
Self-Acceptance, and Healing © 2018

NOTE: Some reviews have been edited for the sole purpose of maintaining the continuity of this literary work.

****

"This book is a wonderful achievement. Beautifully written and deeply honest. The author speaks clearly and with admirable self-awareness about her experiences, people, and events which have (and haven't) helped her cope with her DID. A must-read for anyone interested in this condition, trauma survival, or just in how humans can help other humans. Highly recommended."
Anonymous, 7/21/18

"I wouldn't say it's a 'feel-good' exactly because I was poleaxed with horror many times by the struggles experienced by the author. However, the author's determination to survive and drag the best out of a bad start forms a powerful backbone to this book. This is refreshingly honest. So many books present recovery from trauma as an uphill trajectory (i.e., you say 'yes' to recovery and lo, you are propelled towards healing). This book is more realistic, presenting recovery, not as an intermediate stage between "ill" and "well," but rather as a way of life which will—gradually and with setbacks—make it easier to accept and live with your brain. Above all, this is beautifully

written and a fantastic read! Recommended to all mental health professionals!"
Anonymous, 8/25/18

"Pat shares her journey to build a new life after years of abuse. Her heartfelt and honest account is an inspiration. Pat challenges the lack of professional understanding of both ritual abuse and Dissociative Identity Disorder and shares the strengths of those who have played important roles within her healing process. I recommend this book to both survivors and professionals."
Karen, 8/28/18

"I like how DID is accurately portrayed. It is not dramatic or underrepresented. I hope that a lot of 'professionals' out there make a note of the harm they cause by choosing not to believe those of us who have DID."
Anonymous, 10/30/18

"Through the incredibly transparent telling of her story of healing (which is a lifelong process), the author provides a window into the challenges of living with DID and healing from ritual abuse. The lack of understanding of both ritual abuse and DID in the professional community was discouraging, but those who did work to be informed and chose to care and walk beside the author presented the path we all need for healing: unconditional love. Thank you for being another voice for the incredible strength of children who have survived the evil choices of adults who should have protected them."
Janyne M., 9/5/19

"The author writes clearly and easily about the challenges of personal healing from severe child abuse. I applaud her courage."
A. Merplish, 9/18/19

Dedication

This book is dedicated:

To the memory of **Joyce**, who taught me the meaning of unconditional love.

To **Sara**, whose love and support is always there.

To **Maike**, the first Mental Health professional I trusted who truly "got it."

Acknowledgments

I want to thank the people who came into my life at the right time and enabled me to break free from a lifetime of Satanic Ritual Abuse. Without them, I doubt if it would have been possible.

I am grateful to the people who can accept 'all of us' as we are without being judgmental or fascinated by DID.

To those who encouraged me to write my first book, *Coming Out of the Dark*—especially **Heather Shepard**, whose help and support was invaluable—I thank you. I am humbled by those who took the time to read it and gave me positive feedback.

To the many **Facebook** pages and individuals who shared the book, I truly appreciate you. Holding my first book in print was terrifying and a huge step of courage. So, thank you **ALL** for helping me feel I touched you with my story.

A special mention goes to **Laurie Benoit**, who introduced me to **Angela Edwards** of Pearly Gates Publishing. Thank you for your willingness to take the risk of publishing this book.

My gratitude goes to **Maike**, my Mental Health Worker for over three years, who took the time to get to know "us" and somehow stayed sane when we were all trying to talk to her in the space of one appointment. She truly walked the extra mile.

My thanks are also given to those with DID who have taught me so much and to those who have shared their inner spaces with me.

And, finally, thanks to my personalities who did their best to protect me from the worst of the abuse. Without them, I wouldn't still be alive and functioning.

Foreword

At large, we have the media to thank for improperly depicting the plight of a person with Dissociative Identity Disorder (DID) (commonly referred to as Multiple Personality Disorder). That makes the publication of this book and others like it even more critical in today's misguided society. I will be among the first to admit: My perception of the condition was initially formed based on the sensationalism shown in movies and television. I am guilty of allowing that imagery to shape my preconceived notions about what those who have DID are capable of and how they act.

Through my association with Pat, I have since learned to erase all that I thought I knew and begin anew.

After reading Pat's first book, *Coming Out of the Dark*, I felt I came to know and understand not only her but her personalities as well. At the time, I could not begin to imagine what it took to pen such a masterpiece of transparency…until I connected with Pat myself and encouraged her to delve deeper into her backstory. You might ask, *"Why would you do such a thing? Aren't some things better left unsaid?"* My response would be something I tell anyone who listens:

"There is POWER in your words."

I applaud Pat for this literary work that you now hold in your hands — and I cheer for her loudly from across the waters (I, in the United States; she, in the United Kingdom)! I have no doubt she can hear my constant yells of joy, as I know firsthand that writing this book was not an easy task for her. She and her other personalities had to work collectively to share what they desired to share...some with great reluctance and silence at times. Still, they persevered, and here we are today!

I will forewarn you that some of what you read may shock you. You may find yourself wanting to throw the book across the room in anger (not at Pat, but what she endured). There may be other times when you will cry and hold the book close to your chest as you envision her trying times. Here's the thing, though: She's a **SURVIVOR**! This is her story of healing against all the odds!

Now, I must say this: In getting to know Pat personally, I can attest to her fight to produce something that will not only educate but entertain her audience. She has a fiery way with her words that will leave you in stitches (something I've come to love about her). As you read, I ask that you release all you think you know about DID and simply get to know Pat and her other personalities.

This book is truly a piece of literary art, much like that of a painter who, with every stroke of the paintbrush, works tirelessly to draw you into their world. That's precisely what Pat, Suzie, Trish, Tracy, Heather, Cath, and Anne did on the pages of this book. Their journey to healing isn't easy (notice I used the present tense and did not say "wasn't easy"). Their healing is a continual and daily process. Where you and I can release that "dead and toxic stuff" and move on, Pat is just learning about many of the things that caused her personalities to take up positions of protection in her life — even the youngest one at a mere seven years old.

I encourage you today to pray for Pat as she walks her unique walk on this side of Heaven. Then, when you're done reading this book, anytime she crosses your mind, stop whatever you're doing to whisper a prayer for her. Chances are more than likely she needs your good vibes at that very moment. Why would you deny her that need?

Today, I am very grateful for my U.K. Sister, Pat Suzie Tennent. We have forged a bond that I do not take lightly, especially considering that **ANY** one of her personalities could have easily rejected my sudden presence and purpose in their lives. So, I thank each of them:

Thank you, my U.K. Sister Pat!
Thank you, Suzie!
Thank you, Trish!
Thank you, Tracy!
Thank you, Heather!
Thank you, Cath!
Thank you, Anne!

I extend my arms as far and as wide as they can stretch to embrace you all with the warmest of hugs from across the miles! **YOU DID IT!** This book is the result of now knowing that you *CAN* work together while still maintaining your individuality.

To you, Dear Reader, I thank you for investing not only your money but also your time into this project. You will not be disappointed and are sure to learn **SOMETHING** new! Grab the tissues and your favorite "reading drink," climb into your comfy corner, and prepare to dive into a book that was over 60 years in the making!

Angela R. Edwards, CEO & Chief Editorial Director
Pearly Gates Publishing, LLC
Houston, Texas (USA)
www.pearlygatespublishing.com

Preface

In 2018, I published my first book, *Coming Out of the Dark*. For several years prior to that time, I had kept a journal for my own use. However, a very dear friend, Joyce, asked me to promise I would write a book about my experiences of living with Dissociative Identity Disorder (DID), as she believed that by doing so, I could help people to know they were not alone. She asked that of me less than a week before she passed away. *Coming Out of the Dark* was the result of my promise to her.

In truth, I didn't see myself as an author. I didn't believe nor expect people would read my story. But, as usual, Joyce had more faith in me than I had in myself. Seeing that book in print was a terrifying experience. I had put my story out into the world, all while being unsure of what the consequences would be. After all, my DID was the result of a lifetime of Satanic Ritual Abuse, and I was frightened the group I had escaped from would be able to track me down.

However, by writing my story, I actually confirmed to myself that they no longer had control over me. I was **FREE** to tell my story and take back ownership of my life. I had control, not that group of people.

Moving forward...

I never imagined I would even consider writing another book, but life has a habit of proving me wrong. My journey towards healing has taken huge leaps and bounds since I put the final full stop at the end of *Coming Out of the Dark*. My life has moved on in so many ways. I understand myself so much more and realize the process of healing takes years and years of hard work. It is definitely **NOT** smooth sailing.

There is an increasing passion within me to raise awareness for DID. It is a condition that is so often misunderstood by both the general public and, unfortunately, by so many professionals.

So, just as I was thinking that maybe there was a second book inside me, the universe suddenly sent Angela Edwards into my life. Before I really had time to think, I had signed the contract with her to publish what you are reading at this moment. I am a great believer that we meet people at the right time for the right reason. My first book certainly proves my belief in that statement.

And so, here we go! Book number two!

Introduction

I AM WE is my [our] story of my ongoing process of recovery and healing from a lifetime of Satanic Ritual Abuse. The abuse started when I was a very young child; however, it wasn't until moving with my parents to be closer to my mother's family that the shocking and traumatic experiences involved with that kind of abuse led me to develop Dissociative Identity Disorder (DID).

I have seven distinct and very different personalities you will meet in the following chapters. I will introduce them to you, but when I wrote my first book, I discovered during the proofreading that some of them had written bits of which I was unaware. That makes writing an introduction about what the reader can expect rather difficult.

I do, however, have a broad outline of what I **WANT** to say — but I cannot guarantee who will pop up and say things that are not in my planned outline. I fully expect that when I read the final copy, I will end up with a few surprises.

Nonetheless, I hope that you, Dear Reader, will learn more about DID from the viewpoint of someone who has lived with it (and continues to at the age of 66). It is a condition that is not generally understood very well, and the media has not done us any favors by the way they portray us in films. We are not "dangerous people who have evil ax-murdering personalities lurking in the background." In truth, we are at more danger from other people than they are from us, all because we are misunderstood on the surface. Plus, there's the fact that our experiences of being abused have left us emotionally and physically vulnerable.

Considering everyone with DID experiences it differently, it must be noted here that this is very much my personal story. The language used on the pages of this book is my preferred language. For example, I refer to my other parts as "personalities," whereas others may refer to them as "alters/parts/inners, etc." I think it comes down to personal choice and what people are comfortable identifying with. Personally, I shy away from the word 'alter' because it triggers memories of the Satanic abuse and their use of "altars" in ritual ceremonies.

I will try to explain what living with DID feels like for me and how it affects my daily life — how sometimes, it can put me in danger while other times, crack me up laughing or depress and frustrate me. My hope is to share my personal journey, to include what and who has helped me…and what and who hasn't (there are a few of them)! I believe everyone with DID finds their own way to healing. I am not a professional. Neither am I an expert. I can, however, talk from the heart about my own experiences.

If you are reading this and work in the mental health field, I hope it may help you understand a bit more about DID because training seems to be sparse in this area. For those who know nothing about the condition, it is my desire that you gain some understanding of our lives.

For those with DID, I truly hope my story can show there is a light at the end of the tunnel, which seems to be never-ending. Our personalities were created to keep us sane through experiences that would have (frankly) sent us into madness. I, for one, thank them from the bottom of my heart for their protection.

So, you may be wondering, *"What does healing look like for you, Pat?"* Well, for me, it means being willing to listen to the traumatic memories my personalities hold **AND** a willingness to communicate with them. Above all else, I long to love my personalities, particularly the ones most damaged who never experienced love, only abuse and pain. For me, recovery is through love — the people who have shown me unconditional love and learning to love ourselves, even though our abusers showed nothing but hatred and contempt for us.

Special Note: Although I have written about the last two years in chronological order, I have deliberately left in the somewhat "random" bits. With seven of us being involved in the writing, it was bound to be a bit random…but that is the nature of life with DID!

Table of Contents

CHAPTER ONE

From the Eyes of a 7-Year-Old

AS SURVIVORS OF ABUSE
WE HAVE TO WORK HARD
TO DEVELOP THE THINGS
WE SHOULD HAVE LEARNED
HAD WE GROWN UP
IN A LOVING ENVIRONMENT.

DISSOCIATIVE IDENTITY DISORDER

DEVON

Quotes Creator

My mother was Scottish, and my father was English. They married at the end of the war and returned to England. My mother never accepted living in a rural setting. She gave birth to a stillborn son and, only a few years ago did I discover she also had many miscarriages before my parents adopted me at ten days old.

When I reflect on the first seven years of my life, I think of Suzie. The photographs taken at that time show a cheeky, smiling face—a little girl with bright red, slightly wavy hair with a clear face that soon developed freckles on her nose and cheeks. Looking at those photos, I know they are not ones of me but her.

I, as Pat, have no memories of the first seven years of my life. What I have learned about that time has been from Suzie or, more accurately, her telling of those years to others (i.e., friends or professionals). I have stories my father told me later in life about those times, while some information has been passed on to me from relatives most recently, enabling the picture regarding my past to become clearer.

Suzie's memories of those first seven years are, by and large, happy ones—provided you leave my mother out of the equation. Suzie spent her happy times with my dad, who was one of six brothers and who all lived in the local area. She used to play on the farm with him, visiting the animals and riding the tractor. She also helped with the planting of a small garden at the house we lived in and enjoyed playing in the woods behind the house, especially loving the times when the bluebell flowers were in bloom. She loved hiding in the pigsties with the baby piglets and seeing newborn yellow fluffy chickens. Anything to do with nature and her dad, she loved.

The subject of her mother was completely different. She recalls someone who never gave hugs, love, care, or compassion. Apart from that, Suzie doesn't remember specific things about her. I find that strange, considering she recalls the things she and dad did together with great detail.

The times my Scottish grandmother, aunt, and cousins would travel from Scotland to visit on holiday were not happy times. My grandmother held a high position in a Satanic Ritual Abuse group (something we were unaware of until many years later). It was when they visited on holiday that the abuse started. I think the emotional abuse from my mother had always been there, as proven evident by the lack of nurturing for her child. During those visits (and while my dad was at work), my grandmother and aunt introduced a more sinister type of abuse with sexual overtones. Those actions were witnessed by my aunt's two daughters, with the older one finding it amusing to watch the pain Suzie suffered. It was then that a split occurred. Suzie couldn't cope with the trauma of what was happening to her, so Heather came into being to take the pain. By doing that, it enabled Suzie to live a relatively happy life. With no memories of our mother and those holiday visits, she lived those first seven years doing what she enjoyed. The appearance of Heather allowed her to maintain her sense of innocence.

It was only in the last few years that I heard from a cousin on my dad's side who explained that my mother couldn't cope with having a child and needed a lot of support from one of my aunts. Rumor has it that my mother was not mentally well. That could have been attributed to her having a stillborn and then a series of miscarriages. Or it could have been because she herself had suffered abuse at the hands of the cult. In fact, it could have been a combination of both plus the added pressure of producing a child who would be groomed for the cult. That was the expectation because she was the eldest daughter of my grandmother. Eventually, the position my grandmother held would have been passed to my mother and, in turn, passed to one of my other personalities, Anne. The whole situation was very generational—and it was my misfortune to have been adopted into my mother's family.

The above was already mentioned in my first book, but for those who have not read it, that is a condensed version of our first seven years and how we became drawn into a life of Satanic Ritual Abuse.

CHAPTER TWO

When "I" Became "WE"

> *We were never loved in childhood.*
> *Our challenge is to learn how to love ourselves.*
>
> *Dissociative Identity Disorder*
>
> *Devon*

As for the details of what is involved in Satanic Ritual Abuse, I have never felt comfortable with giving details. I have read books that provide the information some may seek; however, my aim is and has always been to talk about recovery rather than potentially trigger people, leaving them unable to read my story. Perhaps some detail is needed, though, to explain the horrors of what goes on in those cults.

In my case, Suzie was introduced to the perversity of my grandmother as soon as we arrived in Scotland. Our inbuilt fear of insects (particularly spiders) dates back to that time. She was put in a box in a dark cupboard with spiders and other insects left to crawl all over her. She remembers that if she screamed, our grandmother would find it hilarious and laugh wildly, so she learned to keep quiet. She also learned not to cry because that only made matters worse. *I still don't think that Suzie cries.*

After a host of incidents consisting of physical abuse, the sexual abuse started. Suzie was touched inappropriately, had objects inserted into her private parts, and was made to touch our grandmother in ways a seven-year-old shouldn't have to. I don't know where Heather was at this time, other than I am being told by her that she was coping with more extreme forms of abuse. At this point, however, she is unwilling to share with me what they were.

Gradually, Suzie and Heather were introduced into group meetings where the abuse was so horrendous, **several** splits in our personality occurred. The cult meetings were held regularly, with many dates on the calendar being 'celebrated.' The worst times were Easter and Halloween, but there were so many different dates that there was seldom a month without some form of 'celebration.'

With that kind of abuse, there is mind control, manipulation, and the use of mind-altering drugs. Because the abuse was so horrendous (being abused by several people, one after the other), my mind split into a total of seven personalities. The cult took full advantage of it, too. I—as Pat—was totally unaware of all that was happening. I was the person who went to school and lived a life (sort of) daily. My only memories were of the emotional abuse given out by my grandmother, mother, and aunt. However, my life was controlled in the sense of not having freedom to do what I wanted.

Trish, who is 29 years old, also functioned in the outside world. She has long red hair and a temper to match. Looking back, I can see she was our protector and the gatekeeper who held the memories and protected me from them.

Everything about Satanic Ritual Abuse was secret and well-hidden. Members came from all walks of life, with many being professionals in influential jobs. In their non-cult lives, they lived what was seen as "respectable lives." They had families and were pillars of society. In cult meetings, however, they were the total opposite. They enjoyed inflicting pain and performed sadistic actions on the innocent. They dealt in drugs and made films of children being abused. Their control was so great, there was no way of escape, especially when members of my own family held high positions.

I was completely under their control. All of us were. I have no doubt that even if we did speak of the atrocities, no one outside of the cult would believe us. Personally, I couldn't tell anyone because I had no idea what was going on. If Trish had told someone, who would have believed her? She was a 29-year-old personality who, in the eyes of the law and world, did not exist. So, my having Dissociative Identity Disorder (DID) was very much to the advantage of the cult.

Back in those days, Satanic Ritual Abuse and DID were not believed in. It was only around 1995 that Multiple Personality Disorder was renamed DID. Unfortunately, even today, there is still much disbelief. I would just have been called a "crazy child with an overactive imagination." Over the years, "I" became "We." Actually, "We" still are "WE": me, Suzie, Heather, Trish, Tracy, Cath, and Anne. As I mentioned in my previous book, I was about 29 when I first became aware of the existence of Suzie, and in my late 40s when I became aware of the others. Outside of Heather, I have no idea when they all came into being. I do know that Trish (although 29) came into being before that age. She was there when I was in my 20s, but when she actually appeared, I have no idea. Trish has guarded the boundaries between myself, Tracy, Heather, Cath, and Anne very well, although, in recent years, she has allowed some memories from them to come through to me. Did she feel I was ready to hear some of their stories, or had she tired of acting as a gatekeeper? I don't have the answer. She may have felt that since I had support, it was safer to share. The memories that have been shared with me were horrendous and freaked me out. I ended up despising those particular personalities because of what they shared, even though I am aware there are a lot more remembrances to come.

CHAPTER THREE

How and When Did THAT Happen?

DID

NOT HAVING THE WHOLE PICTURE OF WHAT HAPPENED TO YOU IN THE PAST.

WANTING TO KNOW
BUT BEING TERRIFIED TO KNOW

DISSOCIATIVE IDENTITY DISORDER DEVON

For years after discovering the other personalities' existence, I was more than happy to deny them and wished they would go away. I didn't want to hear the truth that 'I' was actually 'we'…but I knew it was true. My life was full of gaps that I couldn't explain. I would also find bruises and evidence of sexual activity that was unexplainable. I suppose I made up my own "reasons" which were acceptable to me – but they were far removed from the truth. There were times my phone would ring at home and, after answering it with a *"Hello?"*, would have gaps in my memory for several hours. When I came back to being 'myself,' I would realize I was in pain. I would then dissociate from the pain and decide I had been watching TV at home all evening.

At one point, I had a flatmate who said I kept disappearing late at night and, when I returned, was in a different state of mind, not acting or sounding like me at all. Since denial has always been my coping mechanism, I thought she was crazy, as I believed I had been at home all night.

The DID mind works to protect itself.

A fairly significant problem with DID is that we often get accused of lying. When my personalities were at a cult meeting, I filled the gaps. What else could I do? When the phone rang, and I lost time, I had to 'think' of what I thought I had been doing. It made sense to me that I was doing ordinary things. Other times I was accused of lying was when I said I had been at home when Trish had, in fact, been in the pub. I had no recollection of being there, but people would say I had been. The times I had slits in my wrist, I would always take ownership of them. Frankly, I didn't know how it happened.

I am sure that with DID, I learned to think pretty quickly in an attempt to cover the gaps by pretending I knew where I had been when I had no idea…to pretend I had bought clothes I had no idea of buying…to think I had thrown out things but had no recollection of doing so…to act as if I knew people when I didn't. I believed that everyone was that way. It was normal! As it turned out, it was far from normal.

Up until 1999, I received no help at all for our condition. There were, however, psychiatrists who one minute said I had DID and the next, said I didn't.

The story of my life between 1999 and Christmas of 2017 is explained in my first book. This is my account of what recovery has looked like since then.

CHAPTER FOUR

The Suddenness of "The Switch"

The demons inside
my head
held me in their
arms
when no-one else
would.

Dissociative Identity Disorder

Devon

So, as I sit here congratulating myself and my other personalities for having survived 2019—the year from hell—I have strange feelings about the first day of the year. I tend to think, *"Thank goodness! I made it through last year, but I think there is a whole new year of disasters out there waiting to happen."* I know it's a negative approach and should try to break that habit. I should try to think that this year (2020) is a year of an opportunity for growth. (I will let you know if I manage that one!)

The last two years since publishing *Coming Out of The Dark* have been challenging in many ways with two particularly traumatic incidents which I will talk about later. But it has also been a time of continued healing and progress. If anyone tries to tell you that recovering from a lifetime of abuse is easy, they have obviously not lived our lives. Nor would I ever wish anyone to have to live through the traumatic experiences that cause DID. Those of us who have it know only too well the challenges we face daily.

At the beginning of 2018, I was struggling with memories coming to the surface—specifically, the fact that Anne had been trained to take over a high position in the ritual abuse group and the memories of how the group punished people who "stepped out of line"…the physical torture that was inflicted, including being given electric shocks. There was intense sexual abuse involving not just children and adults, but animals, too. To say it was all debase is putting it mildly. Tracy, Heather, Cath, and Anne were immersed in that world. I'm aware that Trish is still holding back many of those memories from me, though I sometimes get a flash of a memory. At times, while watching TV, I can see something violent, and it triggers the beginnings of a memory. Then, just as fast, it feels like a shutter comes down to put it to an end. I suddenly switch and think or feel that it is Trish coming to keep the barrier in place.

Because of the above memories, I asked Maike if a bed was available in my respite place. It was unusual for me to make that request. Normally, Maike would ask if I thought respite was a good idea, and I would hang on for another two weeks before I said, *"Yes!"* That practice is not in my best interest, but I am nothing if not stubborn. I tend to think the out-of-control feelings will pass, but time after time, it has been proven that they do not. By delaying the remedy, I am not taking care of myself in the way I should. Self-care has always been difficult, likely because I was abused so much and don't feel I have the **right** to do good things for myself.

That week, while in respite, I developed another abscess. Times of stress cause my body to respond in that way. Over the past two years, I have had several abscesses. Thankfully, over the years, only one has needed to be lanced in the hospital. Doctors and nurses know of my fear of hospitals and tend to be willing to wait for them to burst of their own accord aided by antibiotics. Operations terrify me. Being put to sleep and having people work on my body when I am totally unaware triggers the hell out of me. That response is probably because it reminds several of my other personalities of the times when we were given mind-altering drugs.

Times of stress do not only cause me to switch personalities, they can affect my own memory sometimes in

15

embarrassing ways. I can forget my surname and refer to myself using the surname I had when I was married. I have no idea why I do that, as I separated in the mid-1990s. I get strange reactions when I have to get correct myself. Another example is when I was recently at my mental health office trying to fill in a form. The receptionist suggested I take the form away with me and return it later—"if that was easier." When she asked where I lived, I couldn't remember. A similar incident happened at the bus station when I was so stressed, I couldn't read the destination on the front of the bus. A bus driver asked me where I was trying to get to, and I gave him the name of a village in Scotland instead of the one where I live.

CHAPTER FIVE

There's No Place Like Home

Abuse meant your control was taken away from you. Recovery is taking your control back.

Dissociative Identity Disorder Devon

Quotes Creator

In March 2018, I went to visit my friend Mary in Scotland. It was decided I would stay with her and her husband and not visit areas that would be triggering. It was a good week overall, except for the day we drove to the top of a mountain. While sitting and enjoying the view, we were listening to music. When a song came on called "Going Home," I suddenly burst into tears. I realized then I had lived in Scotland for most of my life and loved the country with its scenery. Sitting there, I realized that nowhere felt like home. What really hurt was that I could never live in Scotland again because the ritual group was still very active. It felt like they had won because I had moved to the other end of the country to get away from them. It didn't make sense to me, though. I had moved away to give myself a chance at having a life and to recover as much as possible. As I sat on the top of that mountain, however, I felt a sense of anger, loss, sadness, and weakness. I felt like a weak person because I had run away and not stood up to the group. In reality, there was nothing I could have done anyway.

I think Trish felt the anger and Suzie, the sadness — the anger because Trish had not been able to stop those people, and the sadness because Suzie loved the wide-open spaces of the landscape. As for me, I felt the loss of my friendship with Mary and her family. Seeing each other only twice a year and talking on the phone are not the same.

During my return trip home, when I changed trains, Trish was feeling desperate and hopeless. She didn't want to be anywhere but home and felt cynical about the prospect of our healing happening at all. I suppose I was feeling pretty negative, too. I couldn't see how I could find a life that was happy and fulfilling after all those years of abuse. How was I supposed to come to terms with it all? How could I unlearn all the negative things I had been taught? If I had been 20 years younger, maybe I would not have felt that way. However, at 66 years of age, I now see that even then, I couldn't envision what recovery looked like before old age caught up with me.

CHAPTER SIX

The Voice of Reason Spoke

ME WHILE BEING ASKED A QUESTION
BY A PROFESSIONAL
CAN YOU REPEAT THE QUESTION
PLEASE?

WHAT IS REALLY HAPPENING IS THAT
I AM DOING
RAPID SWITCHES AND HAVE NO IDEA
IF I AM TRYING
TO ANSWER THE SAME QUESTION
OR IF THE CONVERSATION HAS MOVED
ON.

DISSOCIATIVE IDENTITY DISORDER DEVON

I remember that I started seeing floating heads shortly after my return from Scotland. They were just heads, but their flesh was burnt. I could smell the burning and hear them screaming. What began as one head became several. At first, I only saw them in the house, but then I started seeing them outside, too. Maike asked if I knew they were not real. I knew they weren't, but they were there. I knew that floating, burning heads didn't exist, even though I was seeing them more and more. I was beginning to think I was having a psychotic episode, but Maike said, *"No. The heads are a manifestation of your anxiety."* It didn't make them any easier to deal with, but I could handle her explanation, even if it involved changing my medication to see if that helped.

My answer to the ever-rising stress levels was to finally replace the old carpet in the house. I ordered wood flooring for the sitting room and hallway, and new carpeting for the bedroom. I then realized the hall and two walls in the bedroom needed painting before the carpet was laid. My stubbornness was showing itself again. When life is chaotic, just add more chaos! I knew I was pushing myself too far yet again. I wasn't listening to Maike's suggestion of delaying the painting and flooring and, instead, go into respite. Looking back, I was fortunate not to break a bone or something! Three times, while up on the ladder, a floating head appeared between the wall and me, causing me to fall off the ladder.

By the time the month of May came, and the new flooring was laid, I rang my respite place and booked myself in. I finally listened to the voice of reason.

21

Before going into respite, another woman (who also has DID) and I were invited to give a talk at the Mental Health Awareness Week events. It strikes me as a bit funny that I was in respite trying to calm down but went into the city for the afternoon to give the talk…and then return to respite. Given that I don't care much for public speaking, it was Trish who spoke. It seems she did well. I had written down what I wanted to say, which was pretty much about sticking to the facts concerning DID—how it develops, how it is misdiagnosed, how there are no guidelines for treatment, and other things I explained in my first book. Fortunately, the talk did not give much of ourselves away. Alternatively, I knew the other woman intended to speak from a personal account, so in a way, we had a good balance.

CHAPTER SEVEN

An Unusual Visit to the Optometrist

SURVIVORS OF ABUSE
HAVE AN INNATE BELIEF
THAT THEY ARE BAD,
WORTHLESS,
AND OF NO VALUE.
IT CAN TAKE YEARS TO BREAK
THIS WAY OF THINKING.

DISSOCIATIVE IDENTITY DISORDER DEVON

In August, Helen (my personal assistant) convinced me to get my eyes tested. For months, I noticed my glasses had not been properly doing their job. She went with me to my appointment, as visits with opticians are difficult. People who get too close to me make me very uncomfortable. That appointment turned into a scene from a comedy show.

Each of my personalities has different levels of eyesight. At the start of the exam, when the optician was testing to find the right level of lenses, I got stressed with having a male optician too close to me. I switched, and Trish was there while the left eye was being tested. We switched again, and when he asked if I could read the letters using the prescription for Trish, I couldn't see them well. The poor guy had to start all over again, unable to understand why the left lens was impossible for me to see with properly. With great concentration, I managed to remain Pat for the retest.

Then, we had to do an eye test that required pushing a button when we saw a light inside the machine. The woman called me back and asked if I was ready to play a game of 'Space Invaders.' Helen immediately realized that I had switched into Suzie, who likes nothing more than playing games. All Helen could hear coming from the room was laughter. Suzie was supposed to keep her head still but couldn't stop laughing long enough to complete the test. Three attempts later, it was finally done. The woman who administered the test and the receptionists said they had never laughed so much during an eye test! Trish was trying to cover up the switches by cracking jokes all the time. Helen was laughing and telling me what happened. As for me, I just wanted out of there as soon as possible.

CHAPTER EIGHT

A Lesson for the Therapists

When you have DID and therapist wants you to write down what things you enjoy doing.

Me: give me more sheets we all like different things

Dissociative Identity Disorder Devon

Quotes Creator

Just before Halloween of 2018, my 60 sessions of Cognitive Analytic Therapy (CAT) came to an end. I cried at the final meeting—not because it was the last but because I had a sudden thought that I was sitting in a hospital saying goodbye to someone. It reminded me of when I visited Joyce in the hospital to say goodbye just days before she died. It's weird how situations can trigger memories…

Broadly speaking, I learned a lot in those 60 sessions. I understood trauma in a way I hadn't before and how it affected my daily life. I also learned lots of techniques for grounding and was introduced to the Window of Tolerance diagram. I now have a whole file of articles I can refer to about managing triggers and coping with flashbacks.

I found it difficult to work through the worksheets the therapist gave me. I couldn't just answer the questions from my own viewpoint, as my other personalities wanted to state their opinions, too. I was also aware that the day-to-day stresses of life often dominated the therapy space. We did, however, attempt to explore those stresses in the context of my childhood. So, we tried to work on two levels: processing the trauma of the past and looking at techniques to help manage my immediate levels of distress. (I'm not quite sure if I made real progress with that.) If I had a memory in therapy, she asked if I could leave the memory at the door of the hospital and pick it up the next week when I came to see her. No, I couldn't. In the same way, I couldn't leave the stresses of everyday life outside the therapy room.

During those therapy sessions, I placed a high value on a space where I felt safe. That was in stark contrast to the past, where boundaries with therapists and support were crossed.

I did learn more about myself and managed to gain a sense of assertiveness sometimes, occasionally tending more to my needs. I recall us talking about how me having greater levels of self-acceptance and compassion could lead to a more integrated sense of self. I have a long way to go with that one. My psychiatrist later said I held unrealistic expectations of what I could accomplish in therapy. Perhaps I did. Maybe it was unrealistic to expect co-consciousness to be reached in the span of a mere 60 sessions. To me, unrealistic expectations are better than having none! No expectations would have been a waste of both the therapist's time **AND** mine. But, as our health service can only provide a limited number of therapy sessions, I was frustrated at not making more progress.

I feel I may have made more progress if certain things had been done differently. If my therapist only talked to me, then my other personalities were not getting the space to speak. If they did talk to her, then she always referred to each of them as 'Pat.' Think about it: How would **YOU** feel if someone kept calling you by the wrong name? I know it infuriated Trish, and Suzie got upset.

I also know we were not too happy about being put into "boxes." My therapist used to draw diagrams for me to explain things, and I still have one she drew about all of us. The sheet has boxes, and, in each box, she wrote the characteristics of each of us.

Thus, the sheet says:

> ➤ Trish: Angry, defensive, avoidant, frustrated, willful. Trish keeps the barrier between me, Cath, Tracy, Anne, and Heather, and she knows a lot more about what they think.
> ➤ Anne was in a box that said she was cruel and sadistic.
> ➤ Cath was labeled as hurt, vulnerable, and abused.
> ➤ Suzie: Fearful, demanding, needy, and straightforward. Also, naughty, playful, innocent, sense of humor, and knows secrets.
> ➤ Me (Pat), she listed as the one who is intelligent, talented, creative, has a sense of humor, understanding, compassionate, inquisitive, perceptive, and intuitive but not judging.

Looking at that list, I wonder if that is how it was during my time in therapy. A lot has changed since then. I will certainly settle for her description of me. It makes me seem like an okay person! To put that Anne was cruel and sadistic is not exactly helpful to Anne. Plus, it doesn't seem accurate, given what I know about her now. As for Trish, she probably was just as described during therapy, but again, she isn't that way now. Suzie, she did get wrong. She wasn't fearful, demanding, needy, or naughty…although she was the rest.

I wonder if therapists have preconceived ideas about child personalities and the personality that is the protector. I only know it makes me feel uneasy. I don't think it is as easy as putting characteristics into a box. We are all complete personalities with our different likes, dislikes, and interests. I feel those aspects were not taken into consideration in therapy.

Since finishing therapy, I have thought a lot about what I need in a therapist. My DID was caused by repeated trauma, so I need a therapist who is trauma-informed. Like other survivors, I feel unsafe. I lack trust and live a lot of my life in fear because of past experiences. So, for me, central to recovery is a positive experience of a relationship with a therapist. I need to feel safe mentally, emotionally, and physically with a therapist, as only when I feel those things will we all be able to communicate with him or her. Lack of a feeling of safety means I can't trust, will be fearful, and be afraid of betrayal and rejection by the therapist.

It is also important for me to have choices when working with the therapist so that we can feel empowered, not controlled. Being controlled was a central part of my past. I need to feel respected and to be given information about any treatment plans. I need to be involved in those plans and have them written down for me so that all my personalities are aware of what will happen during therapy. As an abuse survivor, I am vulnerable, and any therapist needs to be aware that taking control away from me can lead to me being retraumatized. I think healing happens in safe relationships where there is a sharing of power and decision-making.

I do, however, understand that many therapists do not usually work with their clients that way. They sometimes do not show very much of themselves in a session, with a tendency to work from standard procedures. People with DID need an individualized approach because we are not all the same. What works for one person does not work for another. I also feel we need a bit longer than the standard 50-minute hour. It also irritates me to be seen as "disordered" or "defective." My symptoms and behaviors are linked to my horrendous childhood experiences. The vital question we should be asked (as I have stated before) is **not**, *"What is wrong with you?"* but rather *"What **happened** to you?"*

Just as in the process of grief, there are stages that survivors need to work through that are not a straight line to recovery. We often think we have dealt with some particular issue, but it later resurfaces, and we have to go back to work more on that issue. That can happen many times, as our minds try to process those issues.

Some therapists try to get us to talk about our memories before we are ready. I think we should not be forced to do that. The therapist should be willing to listen to those things we are ready and willing to share. Because we were forced to do things in the past and to obey when told to do those things, it is vital that the freedom to talk about our memories is ours. Any hint of control can seriously retraumatize a client.

I am well aware that the telling of my story in therapy does not mean the memories will disappear. I don't think they will ever disappear, but I can learn to deal with them better. Perhaps I will never get to the point of not being triggered by certain smells, sounds, etc., but I am determined to learn to deal with those occasions in a healthier way. I can have hope for a brighter future, now that I realize the abuse was in the past and not my present. Still, to me, talking is not enough. I need to do body work, too, to release the memories held in my body and to lessen the tension held there. What worked for me was Equine Therapy. I have also found Tai-Chi helpful. Massage has helped in the past, but only with someone who understood I may need to ask them to stop at certain points or not to touch me in certain areas. In many ways, I feel the loss of the body work I did in Scotland with Sara.

In many areas, choice is vital—not just in therapy sessions. I used to be afraid of smear tests because they triggered memories. I need to be able to ask the nurse or doctor for a break and be able to explain my problem without feeling like I am being difficult. Also, in many ways, it's not just the therapists who need to be trauma-informed; many other professionals do, too. For example, being examined by a nurse who calls me "Sweetie/Darling/Dear, etc." can send me off into a flashback of past abuse. Instead of seeing me as being oversensitive, it would help if professionals were better prepared to listen if I ask them to not use certain words. I know that is asking professionals to work outside of their comfort zone, but I am not being difficult. My problems with lots of things have evolved from my trauma. Perhaps there should be more training in trauma-informed care.

I think, too, that in the U.K., trauma survivors are not getting all they help they need. In my area, service veterans can get service or assistance dogs and have access to Equine Therapy. While I have a great admiration for the men and women who have fought for our country, I do question why someone with DID and C-PTSD cannot access the same services. For me, having a specially-trained dog would be a fantastic help! It has been proven that dogs are of great benefit when it comes to anxiety attacks by placing themselves between the anxious person and what (or who) they perceive to be a threat. In terms of DID, I have read in Facebook groups that trained dogs can cope well with switches of personality and help to ground people when out in public.

CHAPTER NINE

Using "Feeling" Words

If you have been
hurt,
abused,
lied to,
betrayed,
disbelieved,
belittled,
and can still smile

Believe me when I say
you are damned strong.

Dissociative Identity Disorder Devon

A fter therapy was complete, it was just Maike and me who continued the work. I know that during the three and a half years "we" had with her, everyone spoke to her — in person and often by text or email. The messages by text or e-mail were helpful to me, as I could see for myself what my other personalities were thinking or feeling. (Just typing the phrase 'thinking or feeling' made me smile.) Often, Maike would ask what I was feeling, and I would tell her what I was thinking. It took a while for her to explain the difference between "I think" and "I feel." I still wasn't used to expressing my feelings, so it took some time to get the hang of it. Because I had never shared feelings very much, it was a difficult thing for me to do. I'm sure the others found it harder than I did.

Just this morning (as I am writing), I found a letter that Cath had written to Maike. Within, she explained what she was feeling about herself and life, so I will quote it here.

****

I don't understand what is happening. Pat, Suzie, and Trish are all so upset that sometimes, they are all disappearing and leaving me in the outside world. I don't cope well with being out.

On Wednesday morning, it was just me, and I got hysterical. I couldn't phone you because I have not talked to you and don't usually talk in the outside world. I have never lived in the outside world — only in the ritual world — so I don't know how to handle it. I look around and see things I don't understand. The sky and trees terrify me. Actually, everything

I see frightens me. I just don't understand the world or how it works. I don't understand people and how they work. The life I have lived is so utterly different than the life Suzie, Pat, and Trish live.

I feel that all the assaults Pat had to put up with before we came down here were my fault. In the ritual group, I knew things. I knew people and how they worked. I became a danger to the group because I stayed in the area. The group did not know if I would talk or tell Trish, especially. So, the group sent people to terrify Trish and Pat by threatening and assaulting them. The group just wanted to make sure all of us would keep quiet or go back and rejoin the group.

The police and psychiatrists decided it was all in our heads, so the group need not have worried. But I feel guilty that Trish and Pat had to go through the pain that they did. I am angry, too, because the group got away with it. I feel guilty about my life, too. I don't know if my life is worth anything, and I am afraid. I am worried, too, that because of me and the other personalities who have never lived in the world, Suzie, Trish, and I will never make it. I feel stuck because I don't know how to live or even if I want to live.

****

Interestingly, as I typed that, I see Cath used the word 'feel' quite a few times.

CHAPTER TEN

"WE" Chose Our Individual Colors

There is no medication for
DID
but Meds can help with the
PTSD.
However this can cause
problems
as we all react to medication
differently
What works for one of us
sometimes doesn't work for
others.

Dissociative Identity Disorder Devon

I'm not sure when colored felt-tip pens began to be used. Was it my idea or Maike's? Or did it just happen naturally? I do remember that instead of Maike coming for home visits, I started going to her office because there was more room. We used a large table with sheets of paper where we could write. During the process, each of us chose a color, so Maike would know who was communicating with her. Writing seems to have always been a good way to express ourselves. For those of us who did not talk often, we found it easier to write. Not only did we use different colors, but we all have different styles of handwriting.

Our color choices were as follows:

➢ Blue – Pat
➢ Pink – Suzie
➢ Purple – Trish
➢ Green – Tracy
➢ Brown – Cath
➢ Black – Anne
➢ Yellow – Heather

Curiosity leads me to wonder why Heather chose yellow, as she suffered a lot of abuse from my grandmother and her friends. Why did she choose a bright, cheerful color? I can totally understand the choice of brown and black by Cath and Anne. It's interesting, too, that I personally don't like wearing brown, black, or yellow, though we do now have one yellow jumper and jacket in the wardrobe. I do know that black and red reminds us of ritual abuse situations.

I would sometimes write emails to Maike and then, when reading them back, noticed that other personalities had written bits as well. There was one email that was quite long. I remember sitting with Maike, using the colored pens to mark who said what. Often, more than one of us would agree with a statement that had been written. For example, only Trish and I admitted to seeing the burning heads. Was that true, or was it that Cath, Tracy, Anne, and Heather were still lacking in trust? Suzie, Trish, and I thought we had made a mistake by talking our way out of the place of safety immediately after a scary incident with a train. The others made no written comment. The simple fact is that Trish talked her way out of the place of safety by appearing calm and rational. Most of the time, in cases like that (including trips to Accident and Emergency), it is she who does most of the talking, although I am there nowadays for some. Considering Trish has always been known as the "angry one," she can also be extremely calm and rational, even when fury is burning underneath. I think she feels she is protecting us so we can get home.

One day, Trish wrote a page of what she was feeling. As usual, she started by saying she was 'absolutely furious' (it seems she is not too keen on giving up on her reputation of being the 'angry one'). However, she went on to write that she was upset. About what? She said she felt:

- ➢ Invalidated.
- ➢ Scared (a new feeling for her).
- ➢ She wasn't managing to protect us the way she used to.
- ➢ She had come out from behind her barriers, and life had started touching her emotionally.

➢ She was struggling with trust.

➢ She didn't feel like the fighter she used to be.

➢ She felt she was failing every one of us.

➢ Admitting to needing help was making her feel inadequate.

➢ She admitted she never talked to professionals properly when she actually needed to.

➢ She admitted to being tired of keeping the barrier between Suzie and me, and the memories of the other four personalities — that knowing more of our story was 'doing her head in.'

Today, we continue to use colored pens. I tried keeping a journal but found that not all of us were willing to participate. The use of the pens at home turned out to be easier than I would have thought. We could express what we were feeling or wanting by using the pens. For example, over Christmas, there was a note in pink saying that two Paddington films were on TV, along with the times. Because of that, Suzie was able to watch them. With her pen, Trish left a note saying, "*Christmas tree lights only allowed on in the evening, not during the day.*" I would leave notes saying, "*Stop spending money online*" (aimed at Suzie). Trish also leaves notes about what needs to be done in terms of paying bills. Cath, Anne, Tracy, and Heather seldom leave notes, except to express in one word what they feel, which is always negative (i.e., unworthy).

Just before Maike left in 2019, she asked us to write what we would like to do in the future. The answers were both interesting and positive.

- Suzie wanted to:
  - Paint
  - Read comics and fairytales
  - Be on a farm with animals
  - Walk in the woods
  - Garden in a place where she felt safe and could act like herself
- Trish wanted to:
  - Make things, but not sure what yet
  - Do things with people where we can all be "us" safely
  - Go to Wales and go out on the motorbikes
  - Talk about DID to people, such as professionals, who don't know about it
- Pat wanted to:
  - Make friends, as we don't have any here who accept us as we are; we only have acquaintances
  - Move from the area
  - Attend a writing class in a safe place
  - Attend art classes in a safe place
  - Have all of us be friends
  - Do Equine Therapy
  - Go to new places with people
  - Do something on a farm, too
  - Do some kind of exercise
- Cath wanted to:
  - Get out from behind the wall and learn to live in the world
  - Start with animals because they are safer than humans

you will never understand

I don't like you.

- ➢ Tracy wanted to:
  - o Play badminton and golf
- ➢ Anne wanted to:
  - o Learn how to love herself
- ➢ Heather wanted to:
  - o Do some of Suzie's things because, as her twin, she has the bad memories
  - o Do fun things

CHAPTER ELEVEN

"WE" Versus the Train

> *A major problem with having*
> *DID*
> *is that another*
> *personality/alter/inner*
> *can attempt suicide*
> *and you don't even know.*
> **Dissociative Identity Disorder Devon**
>
> Quotes Creator

In October 2018, things were not going well with all of us. I got a memory from Anne that I couldn't cope with. I discovered she had been trained to take over a position in the cult once held by my grandmother and mother. I hated her and wanted her out of my mind, along with her memories. I still don't know all that she was involved in, and although I want my whole story, I am terrified to find out the details. The memory I got was too horrific. I felt as if I was losing the plot big time.

My mind was full of the flashbacks, my stress levels were through the roof, and I truly felt I couldn't carry on with the knowledge I now had. It didn't matter what the professionals told me; I could not accept it. In theory, I could understand that Anne had no choice, that she was brainwashed and controlled, and that it wasn't her fault. If it had been someone else's story, I would have been more understanding, but because it was part of my story, I had no sympathy for her at all. I guess my attitude towards her made things worse. She must have felt utterly alone and unloved — well, *HATED* would be nearer to the truth. I was in self-destruct mode, and Trish was feeling guilty about allowing the memory to surface.

I had always wanted to be co-conscious and to know what happened to the others. I've wanted to piece my life together, but that was a piece I didn't want. I got in such a state, Trish had to take over. She went to the pub for a couple of drinks to give her courage and then took Anne to the railway tracks so she could jump in front of a moving train. (By the process of elimination afterward, I figured that was the course of events. Anne is never out in the outside world, and Trish would have been the only one to have gotten on a bus and taken her there.) The next thing I knew, I was standing under a bridge three feet away from the railway tracks, totally unable to move.

I was frozen in place. I kind of agreed that waiting for a train just might have been the best idea, but then something in me went into a panic. I wanted to move away, but try as I did, I couldn't. I checked my pockets and found my cell phone in one of them. I managed to get my hand to dial Maike, and, thankfully, she answered. For once, she wasn't with a client or driving. I told her I was three feet away from the tracks and couldn't move. She asked where I was—an answer I knew because I already had about four railway tracks I thought of when thinking of ending my life. She told me she was hanging up and would ring me right back. A couple of minutes later, she called and asked if I had seen any trains. *"No, I hadn't,"* came my reply, *"and I still can't move."* She said the police were on their way and kept talking to me. A couple of minutes later, a policeman came running down the embankment, roughly dragged me away from the tunnel, and pulled me halfway up the embankment. (I can't say I was overly impressed with his roughness.) When we made it to the police van, I had a seat on the back with another policeman while the first phoned Maike to tell her I was okay.

I recall both policemen trying to get me to talk and laugh. One of them asked what Maike's favorite cake was because I owed her **TWO** of them. When I asked why, he said, *"Because if she had not taken action so quickly, you would have been dead a minute later because the draft from the train would have pulled you under."* He then went on to explain that he was so rough with me because the train was almost at the bridge. (I didn't even see the train and found that hard to believe.) He said that particular stretch of the track allowed for fast-moving trains to roll through, and they hadn't managed to get the train to slow down enough to stop, hence the urgency that translated to "rough." Apparently, it did stop further up the track, and the driver shouted, *"Is everything okay?"* To this day, I have no recollection of seeing any train in the area. As I sat on the back step of the police van smoking my cigarette, an ambulance approached with its blue lights flashing. I didn't even realize we were on the main road and that in all probability, people from my village were driving on that road. I guess I was in shock but tried doing my usual and act as if everything was calm, at least on the surface. Sometimes, I remind myself of a duck; calm on the surface but paddling like crazy underneath.

The downside of the event was that the police labeled me as needing a mental health evaluation. They took me to a place of safety to be interviewed by three 'professionals.' Then, the warning bells really went off! Being interviewed by three professionals could end up with me being sectioned and put into a hospital. No way! Again, Trish came to the rescue and, after being interviewed, they decided it was okay for the police to take me home. That decision probably had something to do with the shortage of hospital beds, but at least I got to go home!

Another downside was that the police had to take a photo of me for the British Transport Police's records. *I hate having my photograph taken.* Shortly after that was a meeting of professionals, which included the police, to discuss the incident. As I wasn't allowed to attend the meeting, I have no idea what was discussed. It was a professionals-only meeting. When Maike arrived for our next appointment, she gave me the information from the police about what to do should I find myself in the same predicament, along with information detailing that I could be arrested for trespassing on the railway. It was all a bit frightening, considering it wasn't even **ME** who went there.

The experience was a solemn reminder about the dangers of having DID. One personality can decide to kill themselves and all of us end up dying when we all don't want to. I think this fact is especially terrifying for Suzie, who I think is the one who wants to live the most.

The whole situation did nothing for my self-confidence. Even now, it scares me to know that when I am not in charge, I can get myself into life-threatening situations and be totally unaware. For me, this raises the question about mental capacity. If I decide to jump in front of a train, I suppose I do have mental capacity because I am choosing to do it. BUT, if another personality tries to do it, then do I — as Pat — have mental capacity at that point? *It could really be a bit of a grey area…*

CHAPTER TWELVE

The Joys of DID Memory

I GREW UP THINKING THAT WHAT HAPPENED TO ME HAPPENED TO EVERYONE ELSE TOO. I BELIEVED IT WAS LOVE. IT WASN'T. IT WAS HATE. NOW I HAVE TO RELEARN EVERYTHING.

DISSOCIATIVE IDENTITY DISORDER

DEVON

Quotes Creator

Between the end of therapy and the end of 2018, life was rough because of the train incident. At the end of October, I was taken to Accident and Emergency by the police following a discussion with Maike, during which I had expressed ideas of going to the railway line again. I was seen by the psychiatry team and told them there had been a build-up in negative feelings since I was dragged off the railway tracks a few weeks earlier. Apparently, my memories were vague concerning all the events leading up to the police coming to my home.

Actually, having found a letter from the psychiatry team, I am a bit confused. I thought being dragged off the train tracks happened after I finished therapy, not before. Oh, the joys of DID memory! Judging by the letter they wrote to me after the assessment, I wasn't doing too well, although they allowed me to go home after the assessment.

On the 20th of December, I was taken yet again to Accident and Emergency by the police after I left a message with the admin team that raised serious concern. That time, the trigger for my suicidal thoughts was caused by seeing a hearse at the bridge where I had been standing on the railway track. I remember waiting for the hearse to pass through the narrow road, wishing I was in it. So, I panicked.

As I look back at the emails and letters, it seems I have a very unhealthy attraction to trains. That seriously needs addressing, as I didn't realize those thoughts were always in the back of my mind…or someone else's mind.

CHAPTER THIRTEEN

Ideas, Ideas, and MORE Ideas!

> *Never be afraid*
> *to tell your truth.*
> *If just one person*
> *understands and accepts.*
> *Then it is one more.*
> *We can only get our*
> *message of the enormity of abuse*
> *out there by teaching*
> *one person at a time.*
>
> *Dissociative Identity Disorder Devon*

Quotes Creator

At the beginning of November 2018, I met with my psychiatrist and Maike just after the professionals' meeting, which was called after my being dragged off the train tracks. My psychiatrist (who has since left) said I was clearly struggling much more than in the past to maintain a composed and consistent front during the meeting. That shouldn't have been surprising, given the circumstances. During the meeting, however, he did manage to leave me speechless. He was tossing around ideas and bouncing his thoughts into words. He also mentioned the place I went to for respite. When I was there, I felt less hypervigilant, slept better, and had more confidence that I wouldn't get up in the middle of the night and leave as another personality. He wondered what I thought of perhaps being in respite for a year. I think if there had been something close to Trish, she would have thrown it at him. As for me, I was rendered completely speechless!

Eventually, I found my voice and managed to explain that the thought of being physically contained somewhere and not being contained were both equally aversive to me. (There's no pleasing some people.) He then shocked me right back into silence by suggesting a personality disorder service that provided intensive therapy, which involved attending sessions four days a week, though he did not know if I would be eligible for that service. He did say they were just ideas and that he was thinking aloud, but in the process, he successfully terrified me. (Trish, who had been listening (as she does), had a fury later.) He then asked for my ideas on what I thought would help. I don't think he was prepared for the ideas from us—**THREE** size A4 sheets worth! He wrote them down and thanked me for my useful thoughts, so they couldn't have been that bad!

Some of my ideas were:

> To have more one-week breaks in respite.
> Living somewhere safe that was rented because I don't cope well with owning a property.
> Doing work with the colored pens with Maike.
> A proper assistance dog trained to calm anxiety and panic (I can't have one while living where I do).
> Living somewhere with outside space.
> Being able to phone SPA without feeling guilty.
> Having someone to help with repairs in the flat if I have to stay here.
> Not being afraid of police or professionals putting me under a section in a hospital.
> Not being guilty about depending on support. To me, "depending" is a negative word, and it is confusing when people tell me to "use my support system."
> More therapy of the talking type at some point.
> Being involved in the choices about me.
> Something active to do during the weekend, as weekends are really isolating.
> Something that would help me feel less vulnerable (i.e., Have I been out and to where?).

My main idea, though, was Equine Therapy. I have been interested in that for months and found a therapist not too far from where I lived who sounded really good and qualified. I then wrote down all the benefits of Equine Therapy. I felt several of them would help Heather, Tracy, Anne, and Cath in particular. Neither of them place must trust at all in humans.

The benefits of Equine Therapy are:

> It works with trauma and dissociation
> It helps to build trust
> It is safe touch
> Improves self-esteem and confidence
> Horses are non-judgmental; they don't care who you are
> Animals show acceptance and affection
> It relieves stress, anxiety, and depression
> Horses are less threatening than people (to me, they are)
> They improve moods
> They teach about relationships
> They would help with body language and physical sensations
> Working with horses would help with boundaries
> It would improve assertiveness
> Improve social skills
> Horses are less confrontational than humans because they don't lie

Writing about what would help us all was an interesting exercise. Afterward, Maike and I discussed the various points and had a great discussion on what could be resolved and what couldn't. The most disappointing facet was that the National Health Service (NHS) does not recognize Equine Therapy as an NHS therapy. I hunted for some funding to allow me to participate but failed. (I probably didn't know the right places to look.) However, my social worker managed to find a charity that was willing to give me the funding for four sessions.

CHAPTER FOURTEEN

Taking a Stand for Myself

> I DEVELOPED DID AND C-PTSD NOT BECAUSE THERE WAS SOMETHING WRONG WITH ME BUT BECAUSE OF THE WRONG THINGS THAT WERE DONE TO ME.
>
> DISSOCIATIVE IDENTITY DISORDER
> DEVON

Life after the train incident continued, but I have often wondered if I was happy to still be alive. I think I was, but the other personalities had very mixed feelings about it, with Cath and Anne wishing they were not alive. For me, it felt as if I was traumatized...*again.*

Two months later, we somehow managed to get through the Christmas period visiting my cousin. Between the trauma of almost dying and the triggers that always got worse at Christmas, we didn't handle it too well. My cousin felt I was not enjoying being with the family. The truth was I was not handling being inside my own head. I think Suzie is the only one who truly enjoys Christmas, but even she found that year difficult.

Lots of people say that suicide is a very selfish choice — selfish because we do not think of the people we leave behind and the pain it will cause them...selfish because the train driver (in my case) would have been traumatized, as would the passengers.

I am not one who believes suicide to be selfish. When someone gets to that point in their life, it is because they can see no other answer, no other way out. They just want the pain to stop, and they are not in a fit state of mind to think about the consequences of their actions.

Anyway, we managed to get through Christmas and its triggers of ritual abuse memories, and began a new year. It wasn't long until disaster struck again.

At the end of January, I was out for a quiet drink in my local pub. A much younger man came and sat beside me at the bar. Initially, I wasn't concerned about his presence, but when he took hold of my hand at one point and kissed me briefly on the lips, I went into freeze-mode. Old patterns immediately took over, and I found it **impossible** to tell him I wasn't happy with his advances. (For abuse survivors, saying 'no' is incredibly difficult. I am still trying to learn how to do that. I can say 'no' to people I trust, but unfortunately, they are few in number.) At the same time, I didn't think that a brief kiss on the lips would result in what happened later.

He left the pub with me holding my hand all the way to my home. I was feeling pretty threatened by his behavior as we set foot in my house—rightly so, given that within a minute, he had ripped off my top (followed by everything else) and led me to bed. Once in bed, I couldn't move. I felt like a rag doll as he moved me into the positions he wanted me in, telling me over and over that he loved me and was going to "f**k me stupid all night." I have edited out a lot of the details, but the experience was terrifying and rough. Looking back, this was a guy who was angry and wanted to control a woman. I think *any* woman would have done at that moment. My sense of timing is foggy, but I felt like the rape lasted forever. I have no idea how long it went on. Eventually, he went to sleep, and I found the strength to get up, put on my dressing gown, and go into the kitchen. I sat and lit a cigarette, trying desperately to get out of freeze-mode. I was in a state of shock. I didn't say no because I couldn't, but neither did I say yes or even *maybe*. To any man and under "normal circumstances," it would have been obvious I did not give permission.

Eventually, Trish showed up and told him he had to go, which was easier said than done—even for her. He made it obvious he was staying the night and that he didn't even know where his clothes were. Trish collected them from around the living room and dumped them at his feet. Eventually, he left. Trish had come and done what she needed to do, so she left, too. I locked the door behind him and started shaking.

A couple of cigarettes later, I managed to phone SPA (the Single Point of Access service that provides mental health support by phone between 8:00 p.m. and 8:00 a.m.). They told me to call the police because I had been raped, but I couldn't do that. I didn't know what I wanted, but it wasn't having strangers in the house. Instead, I sent an email to Maike detailing what had happened. She came to my house the next morning and said, *"You have two choices: Do nothing or report it to the police."* I chose to report the rape.

All the times I was abused in the past, I truly believed what the cult told me: I deserved it and that being abused was all I was good for. This time, I felt differently. I had been raped by a total stranger and hadn't deserved it. I had been in the wrong place at the wrong time with a man who obviously had control issues when it came to women. For once, I chose to stand up for myself.

Maike rang the police on her cell phone and put it on the speakerphone so I could hear every word (I wasn't capable of talking to them myself). Then, we just waited for them to show up. When they arrived, a policewoman took my statement and bagged up my clothes, bedding, etc. I felt like I was in a nightmare I couldn't wake up from. While she was talking to me, other police were out trying to determine who the guy was.

The following day, a policewoman who worked specifically with sexual offenses took Maike and me to a unit for a physical examination. If I had felt better, I would have been impressed. It was staffed by women who were incredibly supportive and caring. It was explained that everything would be at my pace and if I needed a break, just to tell them. (Looking back, I can easily envision the woman who was going to do the examination being a professional comedian because she kept making me laugh.) So, after more questions, the examination was done. At the end, I almost fainted—which was hardly surprising, given they were taking pictures of both the outward and inward bruising. I didn't want to be touched in that way but knew I had to do it. From there, it was onto another place to give a video statement. I remember sitting in the back of the car eating a sandwich Maike brought with her and asking her to tell me a story. I needed an hour of people just talking about ordinary things to give my brain time to recover before the next bit. Although I cannot remember exactly what Maike and the policewoman said, I do know it helped.

When we arrived, I was shown around the interview room, told where the camera was and what would happen, and then was introduced to the men in the next room who would be recording my statement. I stepped outside, smoked another cigarette, and then went back in to do the interview. I felt I spoke in a non-emotional way and managed to hold it together, but Maike said my eyes were saying it all and showing the emotions. She also told me the policewoman who did the video interview came out of the room with tears in her eyes.

The police told me that since I had provided them with the details, they could arrest my assailant, which I believe they did shortly after dropping me off at home. Roughly ten hours after first leaving my house that day, the police dropped Maike and me back at my flat. Once there, Maike put clean linen on my bed before going home.

It may seem strange, but I distracted myself by spending time on Facebook. On our village's page, people were asking why there were so many police cars in the area on Wednesday night. I mentioned it to Maike, who said, *"It was because of you."* (Sometimes, my brain doesn't put two and two together.) That Friday, the police told me my rapist had been arrested and released on bail for a month pending investigations. He wasn't allowed within 500 meters of the pub or 500 meters of my house. They also said I should continue going to the pub as usual, as I had done nothing wrong. (It didn't feel like that to me. Plus, the thought of going back to the pub frightened me). I was also assigned a dedicated policewoman who rang me, and I could ring her.

Eventually, I took a deep breath and went to the pub, but it felt as if the people who usually spoke to me weren't saying anything more than 'Hello.' The bar staff acted weird, too. Was it true or was it that I wasn't talking to anyone? I do recall that while there, every time someone came through the door, I mentally jumped out of my skin. I had never seen the guy before, so how was I to know who his friends were and who knew what about that night? Walking home alone that night, I was terrified. Could he or his friends be lurking around the corner? Thankfully, I arrived safely.

Disappointingly, although it's been some 11 months down the line at the time of this writing since the sexual assault, I still don't like being out in the village on my own.

CHAPTER FIFTEEN

I'm Thankful She Had My Back

Sometimes you meet someone
who is with you on your journey
for a while and then they have
to leave for reasons not their fault or
yours.
Just life.
But having them for a while makes all the
difference.
Now it's up to us to carry forward what we
learned.
To trust ourselves
but at the same time know we will never
forget the part they played.

Dissociative Identity Disorder Devon

Quotes Creator

The next day, Maike came over, and we went for a walk to get coffee and chocolate cake, I think we both needed something 'normal.' While we were walking, Maike pointed out a squirrel (which Suzie loved), and Maike suggested she draw one for her. In that area, there are only grey squirrels, whereas in Scotland, there are much prettier red squirrels. So, with a little help from me, Suzie drew Maike a red squirrel (pictured here).

That poor woman must have spent about 20 hours with me throughout the Wednesday, Thursday, and Friday after the assault. I don't know of many (if any) care managers who would have done that. Even the policewoman stated she was going to write to Maike's boss saying how supportive she had been. From my point of view, I am so grateful she was there all the way through because I needed someone I knew and trusted by my side. Otherwise, I could not have made it without having a complete meltdown. I didn't feel safe with so many strange people and invasive examinations, and needed someone who knew me well enough to make sure I understood what was happening...someone I could poke in the ribs to let her know I needed a break when I couldn't find the words.

I remember not long after I started working with Maike, she would tell me that 'she had my back.' I had no idea what that meant. When I finally decided to ask, she sent an email addressed to all of us stating what she meant.

She wrote:

➢ I do not judge you.
➢ I will listen when you need to talk.
➢ I will work with you to make sure you are getting the support you need.
➢ I will enable you to make choices in your care and to have control in your life.
➢ I will help you to work through whatever comes your way.
➢ I will always be professional, and we will have boundaries to keep you safe.
➢ I will tell you when I think you need to be in a safe place.
➢ I will use services, such as the police or ambulance, but only at times when I feel there is no other option and to keep you safe.
➢ P.S. I will also be a pain in the ass and make you laugh sometimes but will be there for those times you want to cry.

That definition of her 'having my back' went a long way in helping us to build trust. During the days after the rape, she certainly did 'have my back' — and yes, many times, she was a total pain in the ass!

In my opinion, every mental health worker should have that same approach when working with their clients. For all my personalities, we needed that kind of support where we had choices, were not judged, and were enabled to have control in our lives. They were things we never had in the past. Maike's being a pain in the ass while making us laugh provided a sense of comfort because we knew she would do her best to keep us safe when we couldn't. We needed her to be human, not a person hiding behind a textbook. In particular, we needed to know she would always keep professional boundaries and not abuse us (as some 'professionals' before her had done).

Any therapeutic work I was doing with Maike was temporarily put on hold after the rape. Together, we dealt with the fallout of what happened while waiting for a decision as to whether the assailant would be prosecuted. I remember repeating to people, *"If this case doesn't go to court, I will jump under a train because it would prove the only thing I was good for was being abused."*

I was appointed an ISVA (Independent Sexual Violence Advisor), who explained how the justice system worked. She could talk to the police on my behalf to see how the case was progressing. She also suggested I see Rape Crisis (a charity) to request being put on their waiting list for counseling. I went but discovered their waiting list was about six months long. After my initial inquiry, they informed me they couldn't place me on the list anyway, as they did not have experience working with individuals with DID (I can't say with surety that is true for Rape Crisis in all areas of the U.K., but it certainly seems to be in my area.) To be honest, that response was very upsetting. After all, I didn't want to discuss anything about DID, just about the rape.

Again, I was left feeling as if having DID meant I was being discriminated against.

CHAPTER SIXTEEN

Letters to "US"

Safe connections
and
safe boundaries
are vital as we try to recover
from abuse and trauma

Dissociative Identity Disorder Devon

Quotes Creator

The aftermath of being sexually assaulted was horrendous. Not only did I threaten suicide, but I also blamed myself for the assault. I found I couldn't get angry at the guy, yet I had no problem becoming enraged with myself. I was never good at looking after myself physically, but I took it to a whole new level. I couldn't sleep in my own bed, so I wasn't getting enough rest. I didn't want to take showers because I couldn't stand seeing my naked body. I ate less than usual and wore the same clothes day after day, not even realizing I did so. It was as if I had gone into total self-destruct mode. At that time in my life, I hated everything about myself.

On top of everything else, my stress levels were so high, I lost the ability to talk. I was overwhelmed by feelings of guilt and shame but couldn't see that they were not mine to feel; they should have been my assailant's. As I struggled to piece a proper sentence together, a few words would come out, and then I couldn't finish. SPA was a really good support system on the nights I struggled the most. They gave me the time to try and get out what needed to be said. Helen, my personal assistant, tried to joke about it and say that having silence from my chatter was peaceful. The strange thing was I could *write* freely but not *speak*.

During this time, I started having problems in my flat with water tanks and taps. That meant having a workman in my home, which was the last thing I needed. It didn't help that water is a trigger. My grandmother had a habit of pushing my head underwater until I thought I was going to drown. Hence, the timing of those problems couldn't have been worse.

I hate the smell of cigarette smoke in the house, so I tend to smoke out of my sitting room window. I know, I know: Stopping smoking would have solved the problem of the smell permeating my home, but why give up on the vice of a lifetime? My house is not far from the railway track, so I heard the trains as they came and went. I heard so many, I'm not altogether sure if some were a figment of my imagination or not. Some likely were because I don't think a train happened to pass every single time I smoked.

Then, I started hearing a male voice that told me to kill myself. I don't have male personalities, and that voice was coming from outside my head. Maike suggested I give antipsychotics a try. (I can't say I was impressed with that idea.) We tried a small dose first, which was to be increased daily. That didn't work. Some years prior, I was put on some medications that caused inner chaos — probably due primarily to Suzie. You just can't put a seven-year-old on strong medication without consequences. The poor child felt like she was hit over the head with a sledgehammer! One thing I have discovered over the years is that if Suzie isn't happy or off her head on medication, it has the effect of making none of us happy.

Shortly after that experience, Maike suggested we all write letters to ourselves about what we thought about the rape. I will share mine first:

****

Dear Pat,

Your head is in a mess, and you are being irrational. It is full of emotions that are banging around. You feel guilty, worthless, full of shame and fear, and you hate yourself. So, why do you feel guilty? Because you blame yourself for what happened with that guy. You are guilty because you can't get yourself together. You are guilty of needing help. What about the worthless bit? That feels difficult to answer because it's complicated. You are always told you are worthless. That guy brought it back. That night makes you feel worthless in the here and now. You were not a person to him; just someone he could f**k. You are a nothing, just like you were always told you are. You are told your own birth mother did not want you and your grandmother made it apparent she didn't want to accept you as family.

The way people are reacting is making you feel worthless and unwanted, too. Your birth mother told you that you were the product of her being raped, and now you get raped. It has left you feeling dirty, ashamed, used, and disgusted. You feel you deserve to be treated like that because it's triggered into the past. You are scared. Scared because it's different circumstances from Scotland but the same result. Or maybe you're putting a different label on it this time. In Scotland, it was abuse. This time, it was rape. Rape seems like a strong word somehow. I am scared that if the case is dropped, you will feel that it confirms you're worthless and guilty. No matter what anyone says, you will feel that way. It's okay for people to do what they want to do to you, but you have no protection or no way to prove that he was guilty. So, you get angry with yourself because it was your fault and, if it was your fault, you don't deserve help or understanding. You feel you deserve to be punished, not him.

Actually, you're doing a pretty good job of punishing yourself. Your eating habits are the worst they have been since you moved here, you won't shower properly or change your clothes, etc., etc. You are totally beating yourself up and not interested in anything. You don't want anything to do with your body because you hate it. Actually, you hate your mind, too, because it's spinning out of control. You want to cut your wrist to stop the pain, but you know it won't release enough of the pain. You try to make conversation with people in the pub, but it feels like they are silently saying, *"How dare you accuse a customer of rape!"* That makes you angry and upset. Again, it's all my fault. None of this is his fault, even in my own eyes.

So, you try to push away the people who are trying to help because you think they will reject you, too. Your trust is wobbly. You need to trust the people on your side, but you are afraid, so you lash out and say stupid things, trying to reject them. The next minute, you are scared they will walk away — especially the professionals. You want to tear yourself apart as the ultimate punishment.

Your thoughts of trains lead you to the guy who jumped in front of the train on the way to Scotland that you were on. You recall sound of his body being smashed to bits. That's what you want all the time; that kind of destruction for yourself…to destroy your body so it doesn't exist anymore and so that you won't be hurt anymore sexually by those around you.

****

Trish wrote:

I am doing my head in since I moved down from Scotland. I have begun to feel emotions and to trust. I don't know how to cope with that. I am furious that I couldn't kick that guy in the balls, and angry that I left Pat to cope with it until the last minute. I am furious with what certain people said to Pat. *"Why didn't she slap him, and it wouldn't have happened, etc.?"*

I feel weak instead of strong. I enjoyed going to the pub talking to people. I thought they were okay, so now, I am furious I got it so wrong. I used to be able to figure out people, like who was fake and who wasn't. Now, I don't seem able to do that. It makes me wonder if I ever could.

I'm really struggling with trust and, therefore, struggling with myself. I thought it would be okay down here, but it's not. I am trying to cope with the past and the present, but am failing to cope with either. I hate Cath and Anne and want to destroy them. I want to destroy me. I have failed everyone. I am supposed to protect Pat. I am angry with Suzie for being the one who stops me from jumping in front of the trains. Her innocence and trust drive me mad. I could shake her and tell her to wise up. This life is crap, and I am tired of fighting.

****

Anne wrote:

It is really difficult for me to read that Pat reported the rape to the police. It's hard to know they all hate me, as I hate myself enough as it is.

****

Cath wrote:

Just goes to prove none of us are worth anything, and I know that probably more than anyone. Things like this happened before and happened since we came back to England, but not many of us know that, as those who know haven't told the others—especially Pat. She may suspect but has blocked it.

****

Suzie wrote:

Dear Suzie,

You are sad because you were there that night for just a tiny minute, and it was hurting. I wish I hadn't been there. Now, I can't do the things I like. I don't want my chocolate milk or cookies or cakes. I am unable to help Pat shower or put food in the microwave.

Maybe they are right, and I should not stop them with trains. I'm mixed up.

****

Heather wrote:

The bad thing that happened to Pat makes me think of the bad things that were done to me when I was small. Big people did sore things to me.

****

Tracy had one word to say:

BASTARD!

****

I am aware that I have spoken more than I intended to about that incident. Although it was horrendous, I think what all my personalities wrote actually helped me to understand them. They weren't just talking about that one incident; they were expressing what they had felt about the previous abuse, too. Having them communicate their feelings was them opening up to me. They could have just written to Maike and destroyed the letters, but they didn't. They left them for me to read.

CHAPTER SEVENTEEN

Respite's Safety

> *There is no force more powerful than a survivor determined to rise from the ashes.*
>
> *Dissociative Identity Disorder Devon*

Quotes Creator

In early January 2019, I was messing around on the internet (where I seem to spend much of my time) and started looking for Retreat Centers similar to the one Joyce ran in Scotland. I'm not sure why, because I wasn't feeling overly spiritual. I found several in my area that would have been easy to get to, but none of them appealed to me. Plus, they were expensive. When I changed the wording in the search engine, a location in Wales came up.

I viewed their website and fell in love with the place! It was in the middle of nowhere and run by a couple called 'Joy and Robert' who had a holiday cottage attached to their house. It appealed to all of us. It was in the middle of nature, overlooking a mountain. They had alpacas, chickens, ducks, geese, cats, and dogs. I immediately emailed Joy to ask about the cottage and pricing. We decided to state upfront that we had mental health problems, just in case something went wrong if we went there. We didn't much fancy the prospect of one of us having a meltdown in the middle of nowhere with people who didn't want anything to do with mental health.

Almost immediately, I received a lovely email response. It turned out that Joy had experience in the mental health field, having run a place that supplied respite not very far from where I live! She went on to explain they had moved to Wales about seven years ago and set up home in that lovely area, renting out the cottage for holidays. I made plans to go and visit, but it involved riding three different trains. I was a bit unsure about the traveling and about being in the middle of nowhere with strangers next door. Also, we would have to cook for ourselves while staying in the cottage (we hardly manage food in a kitchen we know, so that was concerning for me). I put my decision on pause.

It was only when Maike said she was going on holiday the first week of June that I started thinking I really needed to be somewhere safe. The cottage in Wales came back to mind, so I sent another email to Joy asking if the cottage was available. It wasn't—but she had a proposition for me. They have never had a guest stay in their house before, but she felt I needed to be there. She had spoken to her husband, and he was willing to give it a try. So, I booked the tickets, organized assistance from the railway company to get me from one train to the next, and Helen drove me to the station. Assisted travel is great because when I get stressed, my rapid switching means I can't read departure boards and would, in all likelihood, end up on the wrong train.

When we arrived at the station, though, I decided that 2019 really had it in for me. The trains were all delayed because someone had jumped in front of one just south of my station. I was put on a train I wasn't booked for and, therefore, my assisted travel people didn't know what train I was on. I got as far as Bristol but couldn't read the departure boards to see when my next train connection was. The station was busy with people and trains everywhere, so I headed for the exit to try to calm down. While sitting on a bench and shakily smoking a cigarette, I realized if I went back inside the station, there was every chance one of us would step in front of a train. Total panic set in, and I was afraid one of us would wander off into the city and get totally lost. At that point, we couldn't even think straight enough to phone anyone.

I then noticed a couple of British Transport Police standing not far from me, so I approached the female officer and asked to speak with her. I must have been in a seriously confused state to choose to talk to the police! Fortunately, she was very nice, and I was completely honest. We spoke for a while and then went into the station to find out when my next train was scheduled to leave. One of the station staff and she got me onto the train, which was not due to leave for 20 minutes. As I sat in my seat trying to calm down, I noticed the policewoman remained on the platform. In no way did she have to worry about me getting off that train. When the train pulled out, she waved goodbye to me. I wonder how many people get waved off by a policewoman! Every station after that, when the train stopped, the guard walked past the window and smiled at me. At one point, I began to feel somewhat embarrassed because of the attention given to me. The next change of trains was accomplished without incident because by then, the assisted travel knew where I was.

After an eventful journey, I finally arrived. It was strange that Joy and I recognized each other. Although I knew it was her somehow, I still walked past her because I expected her to be waiting outside the station. When we got to their house, it immediately felt right. Everyone was happy there, and Trish was absolutely delighted to see the contents of one of the sheds: a motorbike and a Harley Davidson trike. She thought she was in Heaven and could have ridden off on the trike right then, except the keys weren't in it. Just as well, given she hadn't ridden one in years — and certainly not one that big! Suzie was in Heaven with all the animals around but got upset that the alpacas wouldn't talk to her. Joy said that was because she kept calling them 'llamas.' As for me, I just loved the whole place, even though it rained nearly every day. When it wasn't raining, we sat outside with coffee and looked out over the scenery. Suzie had her little bear with her and introduced him to Joy. Both she and Trish chatted happily with her. Trish found books about Native Americans and loved reading about them. It was physically comforting to have the dogs sit at my feet. There is something very therapeutic about stroking animals. They all seemed to like me, too!

Joy does healing and asked if I wanted a healing session. I said yes but was still too stressed out to get the benefit from it. Physically, I was still feeling raw and couldn't cope with another's touch, even though it was a healing touch. Inwardly, I pushed it away. Joy said what I really needed was tender loving care and to relax being away from things.

Oh! One other significant bit: Joy is an amazing cook, and Robert makes lovely hot chocolate in the evenings. I think I ate more during that first trip than I had for weeks before! We all felt comfortable and had some great conversations. Joy and Robert were easy to be around.

I had only booked myself for three nights to see if I liked being there. It seemed like by the time I arrived, it was time to head back home. I knew, however, I would return—and so did Joy and Robert. They said that the next time, I would continue to stay with them in the house, not the cottage.

CHAPTER EIGHTEEN

Justice? What is That?

> *Our minds are full of bad memories.*
> *You know...the ones we would like to forget but can't.*
> *The ones that haunt our dreams and affect our lives.*
> *How about we try to make some new memories for ourselves.*
> *Something little every day that makes us happy.*
> **Dissociative Identity Disorder Devon**

Quotes Creator

Eventually, the police were asked not to ring me directly but to communicate any updates to my ISVA or Maike, as the police's decision was taking too long, and I was really getting stressed out.

I was scheduled to see Maike on her return from holiday and also after my return from Wales. Part of my reason for going away when Maike was away was that I was afraid the police would forget our agreement and come and tell me their decision when I was alone. She rang to tell me that the investigating officer was coming with her, but she didn't know the decision. A sense of unease came over me. I knew…

The officer said they did not have enough to take the case to court. My assailant admitted to having sex with me but said it was consensual (his definition of 'consensual' was obviously completely different from mine). On the other hand, he was highly unlikely to say, *"Yeah, I raped her."* Unfortunately, that meant it was his word against mine, and because he admitted to having sex with me, the forensic evidence could not be used. The investigation officer said they believed me and that they were sorry, but very few rape cases actually made it to court.

I remember thinking, *"What should I have done? Invited a witness into my home who could say it was rape?"* Although it was a thought, I was so upset, I may well have said it aloud. I was also left with the feeling that my having DID didn't help.

The police had asked me if I would have been up to being cross-examined in court. Of course, I would have. I knew the truth, and so wanted the chance to tell it. I could have appealed the decision and had different officers look at the case again, but by that point, I knew I couldn't go through all the waiting again to likely have the case come to the same decision. So, I accepted their ruling and tried to move on (pretty unsuccessfully, I might add).

Some questions remain that I have considered time and again, such as:

Would I have reported the rape had I known that very few cases go to court? *Probably yes.*

Would I advise people in my position to put themselves through that? *Probably not.*

Do I think the justice system is good and fair? **Definitely not.**

The whole subject of rape is a difficult one. Someone said to me, *"Why didn't you just slap the guy and then it wouldn't have happened?"* If I could have, I would have. Victims act differently. Some fight back and end up being hurt more. Some think by not fighting, it will be over sooner. Some (like me) behave like a rabbit caught in headlights. It seems to me the victim gets blamed, no matter how they react.

More cases of sexual assault and rape are being reported, yet less are making it to court. There is something seriously wrong with the system, and the assailants know it. Women are not being listened to and not being given a chance to have justice. Now, I have nothing whatsoever against the police who supported me through everything, but the CPS (Criminal Prosecution Service) leaves much to be desired in my eyes. And no, it does not help me to know that it is on record that I reported the guy for raping me. If he, for example, is pulled over for a driving offense, it will flash up on the police's computer…and then what? And no, it doesn't help to know that if he does it again and is reported, the police will come back to see me. I somehow think he will be keeping a low profile when it comes to women for the foreseeable future.

SIDEBAR: As I sit editing this chapter, it is **exactly** one year from the date of the incident. As much as I try to distract it, my mind is reliving the whole experience. I have been having flashbacks and body memories but have given up on using distraction techniques. Instead, I have decided to sit with the memories that are coming. By doing this, I feel I am perhaps processing it rather than trying to ignore it.

It's been a year, and I am glad I reported it, even though it didn't get to court. I am proud that I did decide to report it. It meant that somewhere, I felt I was worth something and that what happened was wrong. I had the right to say I was raped and didn't deserve it. To feel that way was actually a huge step for me. All my life, I felt I had no right to say, *"This is wrong!"* Instead of keeping quiet (for fear of being disbelieved), I spoke up and was believed. Yes, it would have been good to have justice and for him to be prosecuted, but would that have made me feel any better about it? Maybe not. Maybe the stress of a court case would have added more trauma as timewise, it would have dragged on for many, many months. I know the truth of what happened. Perhaps that is the most important bit for me. I have moved into a new position in my recovery. My body belongs to me, and I have the right to say, *"Hell no! What you did was wrong!"*

CHAPTER NINETEEN

Then, the Other Foot Dropped

> *If a person says something with their mouth*
> *but*
> *something different with their eyes*
> *I will believe what their eyes say*
> *every time.*
> *The mouth can lie*
> *but eyes don't.*
>
> *Dissociative Identity Disorder Devon*
>
> Quotes Creator

It was great to have that time away from my village before facing the police's decision. Physically, I felt better than I had in a long time, after having eaten and rested well. In many ways, I was better prepared for the police when they came to tell me the case would not be going to court. However, I still fought with the idea that the decision would result in me taking my own life because I couldn't get the justice I so needed and deserved. We all felt that way.

I also know that people were concerned about my safety. All my professionals know there is a difference between me saying, *"I feel suicidal"* and *"I am going to do something."* A couple of months ago, a professional totally understood me. She said that when I felt suicidal, it was because I was so distressed that I couldn't find the words to express my distress. That felt right to me. In essence, there is a huge difference between me saying, *"I feel…"* and *"I am going to…"*

After the police's decision, I really fought the urge to return to the train tracks, and Maike knew that.

The following week, Maike came to see me. She said she needed to talk to me. The look on her face reminded me of the time several years ago when Joyce said she had something to tell me, and she told me she had cancer. I was expecting to hear that Maike was ill or something similar. I was not expecting her to tell me she was leaving her job in six weeks.

After knowing her for over three years, I quickly realized her departure was not something she wanted. Questions floated around my mind:

Was she ill?

Was one of her family members ill?

Had she reached burnout?

Maike was the consummate professional. Whatever her reason for leaving was, her primary concern was for her other clients and me. I must admit that when she left that day, the emotions of the past six months all came flooding out. I sat and burst into tears, unable to get them to stop. They weren't tears from just the prior six months either. I was hysterically crying and out of control. It felt like all the tears I had never cried suddenly burst through my self-imposed defense system.

How was I going to deal with her leaving us at such a crucial point? If our relationship had come to an end because our work together was complete, it would have been so much easier to cope with it. I would have been in a position to deal with things myself.

How was I supposed to handle the police's decision?

How would I keep myself alive?

How could I keep hanging onto hope when it felt that everything was falling apart?

Suzie was beside herself with sorrow. Trish was fighting her emotions, trying not to let them out but failing miserably.

I saw Maike every week before she left and counted down every appointment. Because we knew she was upset, for whatever reason, we tried to hold it together. We tried not to complain when we spent four of those six appointments updating care plans and doing paperwork. She stressed the importance of completing the paperwork so that my care continued in the right way.

Part of Trish wanted to tell the mental health services to go to Hell. She couldn't see herself starting all over again, trying to trust another care manager. Cath and Anne felt shattered. They were just beginning to trust Maike and communicate with her, even though most of it was done in writing rather than face to face. Tracy and Heather couldn't see how they could trust a new care manager when it had taken them so long to trust Maike even a little. We all have different levels of trust. I think Suzie and I were the ones who trusted Maike the most.

On July 1st, we had an appointment with Maike and a social worker. The social worker was assigned to complete my application for funding, which was about to run out. She seemed kind enough but at that point, I was ready for the application to be turned down. None of us could see anything positive in life at that time.

During the last six weeks of having Maike in our lives, we all tried various methods of reducing the stress we felt. Trish decided she was paid to care about us, as she was a professional, and all the words, she said, were false. That didn't work, though, as she knew it wasn't true. Cath, Anne, Tracy, and Heather decided no one could be trusted because Maike was just up and leaving us. They knew that wasn't true either. Suzie tried to get angry because she had no one to throw her little bear at, but she found it impossible to get angry. As for me, I knew there was a reason she was leaving that I didn't know, so I tried to be calm and sort of supportive by not having meltdowns while with her. I also knew I would miss throwing the bear. We have had this little bear for about 20 years. He travels with us and has his picture taken each time. I remember him having his photo taken in Edinburgh while sitting on a piper's bagpipes. Sometimes, the person with us gets embarrassed, but that is their problem. That same bear was always at appointments with Maike. He helped us to communicate. If she said something one of us didn't like, we would put the bear's paws over his ears. If one of us didn't want to or couldn't talk, the bear would wave at her. Lots of times, instead of reacting verbally, we would toss the bear at her. It worked both ways in that sometimes, the bear would be tossed at me by Maike or, if I was getting upset for no reason at all, she would use the bear to wave at me. It may sound dumb, but that bear was a useful therapeutic tool.

I tried to think Maike had lots of other clients who must have felt the same way as us (honestly, I didn't care deep down about them, as I was more concerned about me). I suppose on a superficial level, I did care about them…a little.

CHAPTER TWENTY

The Relaxing Sounds of Joan Baez

Do you know what is amazing?

We were never loved in our
childhood.
Quite the opposite.

But survivors
are some of most
caring and loving people you will
ever meet.

Dissociative Identity Disorder Devon

Quotes Creator

My friend Mary came down from Scotland for a week on the 23rd of June 2019. While with me, she asked if she could write to Maike because she was so concerned about me. My mood during that week was not being helped by the fact I had a mouth abscess and was on antibiotics and painkillers. There we were, thinking we would have days out with Mary and eat nice meals. I felt terrible and chewing hurt my mouth. It's just as well that she was there, as I had so many pills, I couldn't keep up with what I was taking. I didn't know if anyone else had taken a painkiller or antibiotic, so Mary's being there kept us right and reminded us of the dosing schedule. Taking medication and having DID has always been a problem. Am I taking the right amount at the right time? Is one of us taking them at all? Or do I have someone who throws them in the trash so we have a medicated trash can and a not medicated me?

Mary said I wasn't talking to her in the way I usually did and that I was really agitated. Anytime someone rang the doorbell, I yelled at them. A man came to read the electric meter, and it seems I yelled at him rather impolitely. When the doorbell rang later that morning, I apparently screamed at Mary, *"Who the hell is that now?!"* — not realizing it was Maike. Mary was also concerned that I was switching so much, I was forgetting to do the simplest of tasks. She explained I would get up during the night and wander around the flat, unaware that I was doing it. She pointed out that we were unable to be out as much as we had planned because it was too difficult for me to make choices as to where to go. I think the thing that concerned me the most was the wandering around the flat in the middle of the night.

While visiting, Mary and I ate in the local pub a lot. Her job is as a cook, and I don't cook, so we had our evening meals at the pub. She pointed out how my body was reacting to the stress I had been under and that my muscles were very tight. I wasn't sitting in a relaxed position; instead, I was hunched over the table and every time the pub door opened, my eyes immediately looked to see who had come through the door. No matter how I tried, I could not get my body to relax. She mentioned I was the same at home. The only time I seemed to relax was when she suggested I put on a Joan Baez DVD. We would both sit on the sofa with her arm around my shoulder. She said she could feel me relaxing. Obviously, I need Joan Baez in the flat singing, as her voice seems to relax and distract me.

CHAPTER TWENTY-ONE

Laughter and Sadness Balled Up in One

When we first started to recover from abuse it was like being stuck in a car in a very tight parking space. We couldn't see a way out. There was too much to deal with, too many emotions, so much fear. We felt worthless. We questioned whether recovery was possible. But like the stuck car we realised it would take time and effort. Moving slowly forward, then going back again. Dealing with what we saw in the rear view mirror. Moving forward again. Recovery is like that. Moving forwards, moving back. But the more we keep manoeuvring we change from victim to survivor and closer to the life we want. A life that is ours, free from control.

Dissociative Identity Disorder Devon

Days after Mary went home, I had my final appointment with Maike. Until the moment she walked through the door, I was terrified she was going to cancel because she had taken ill or something. When she arrived, she carried in her hands four cupcakes: two chocolate and two different flavored ones. Suzie saved the chocolate ones for later.

(During phone calls with SPA afterward, they kept asking if Suzie had eaten the chocolate cupcakes. She hadn't, as she felt when she ate them, Maike would have truly been gone. SPA kept checking and asked me to look at the use-by date. They suggested I wrote it down so that Suzie knew she had to eat them by a specific date. Eventually, she consumed them, but eating two cupcakes and crying at the same time was hard for her.)

Our last appointment was filled with a mixture of laughter and tears: laughing about the funny things we had been through, talking about what we had done together, and discussing how much she had learned from me — not just what I had learned from her. She reminded me how far we had all come over the time of working with her. We reminisced about how I didn't like her when we first met and how it had taken months for me to begin trusting her. Then, she was gone.

When she left, I just couldn't shut the door behind her. I was not into having another dose of hysterical crying, so I went down to the car with her, based on the hope that I wouldn't cry in public. We failed miserably on that one. When I bumped into the housing manager (I live in retirement flats), I promptly burst into tears on her, followed by crying on Helen.

For someone who really does not cry, I was getting pretty good at it!

Since Maike didn't know who would be around for the final appointment, she wrote a letter with a paragraph designated for each of us. Reading it gave me more practice in more crying. As I write this, I just had another look at the letter, which I am not going to quote here because it is personal to us all. I will say that she got it completely right, saying precisely what each of us needed to hear. I just laughed, though, because in reading the bit she wrote to **ME**, she said she thought writing another book could be therapeutic! She also suggested to Suzie that she showed the rest of us the fun in life. The general message was that we had all taken a leap of faith to communicate with her. Now, we had to continue our journey with someone else. She encouraged us to take that leap again and engage with new professionals. I think that being able to work with her for over three years taught me that we were all capable of trusting a professional. If we could do it once, then we could do it again.

CHAPTER TWENTY-TWO

ANOTHER Care Manager? NOT!

*Some people just lack
the courage, patience
and understanding
to hear our stories.*

*This leaves us isolated in our recovery
after being isolated in our abusive
situations*

Dissociative Identity Disorder Devon

Quotes Creator

The shock of the police's decision and Maike leaving resulted in me losing my voice again, either for short periods or days. I was dissociating much more. It must be noted here that I dissociate daily, but there was a period when only Suzie was around for several days. That is hard and frightening for her because at only seven years old, she doesn't cope well with being in charge all alone for days at a time. She gets afraid of something going wrong in the flat, and she can't go out on her own, so she feels alone and miserable. It was during those days that she managed to phone SPA for the first time and said who she was. Thankfully, the person she got on the other end of the line was friendly and chatted with her so that she didn't feel so alone. Trish, however, wasn't happy to discover Suzie had done that. It's not fair of Trish because she can phone SPA without saying it is her, as she sounds similar to me (unless she is angry about something). Trish has a habit of making Suzie feel like she is silly, whereas she is far from it.

My ISVA stayed around for a while longer than she needed to so that I had someone to talk to. My last appointment with her was on July 23rd. During that time, she completed a form for me for criminal injuries compensation. She explained that since I had reported the rape to the police, then I was entitled to victim's compensation. I have weird thoughts about that. In my head, compensation feels like I was paid to be raped. Plus, what on earth would I do with any money? I couldn't use the funds for house improvements, as that would always remind me of where the money came from. It was hard enough living in the flat having flashbacks without walking into a new kitchen (for example) and thinking, *"Oh, my rapist paid for that."* Compensation was the least of my concerns.

After Maike left, immediately getting a new care manager didn't quite work out due to staff shortages. As well, because having DID is seen as being complex, it was thought I needed a Grade 6 care manager, and the only person available was a Grade 3. Personally, I am not into 'grades.' Yes, a Grade 6 is more experienced, but to me, what matters the most is the **relationship**.

Anyway, I was appointed a new care manager in mid-September. My first appointment with her was during the last week of the month. After seeing her about five times, I found out she was leaving for another position just three months after having been on the job. No, we did not scare her away. She got the chance to obtain a job she always wanted. So, after trying to build a relationship with her, **she** disappeared.

The new one I was allocated is on holiday until after Christmas. I'm unsure when I will see her because the appointment she set is on a day when I will be in respite in Wales. I am hopeful this one will not suddenly find the job of her dreams within months of our meeting…

The lack of a care manager and regular contact with someone was causing difficulties. I felt (and still feel) the lack of therapeutic input is making my mental health deteriorate. Thank goodness for SPA. They are people I can dump my thoughts on and calm down when I am getting too stressed. In fact, I rang them last night (December 28th) for the first time since before Christmas. The Christmas holiday was bad for me. I somehow lost so much time, and I didn't know what day it was (or what planet I was on).

This Christmas, there has been some cooperation between Trish and Suzie. Suzie got to put up her Christmas tree, although Trish seems to be only allowing the lights to be switched on in the evening. That's significant progress, as Trish will usually put the tree away as soon as it goes up. I think it's particularly hard over Christmas because of the memories of ritual abuse and not getting presents — well, not presents of a good kind. We received gifts of the abusive kind.

Perhaps writing this book over the holiday period is our distraction technique. I realized I finished writing my previous book over the holiday period at the end of 2017, so there may be some truth in that.

CHAPTER TWENTY-THREE

My Gratitude for Helen

We get taught lots of different
distraction techniques.
And yes they have a place.
But I wonder if we should use them
every time we have a panic attack,
have flashbacks, uncomfortable
emotions.
If we distract all the time are we
in a sense trying to bury
the emotions we need to sit with
and feel in order to heal.

Just a random thought from my
wandering mind.
Dissociative Identity Disorder Devon

Quotes Creator

There were lighter moments during that time. Not many, but some! My personal assistant, Helen, provided a lot of them. There was one time when I had bought two tickets for the final U.K. tour of Joan Baez at the end of February 2019. I had no idea who would come with me, as it was in Cardiff, Wales — *a two-train journey.* There was no way I was going to miss Joan's final concert! Helen graciously offered to come with me.

On the way there, poor Helen had some problems with me. I was looking out the window at train tracks until she distracted me with a crossword puzzle. Then, when we arrived in Bristol, which is a fairly large train station, I started dissociating. One of us began to stare at the trains coming in and out of the station, and I felt an inner pull to step in front of one. Thankfully, Helen knows me well enough to recognize the signs and stood between the railway tracks and me, telling me to look at her because I was not about to die on her watch.

We made it to Cardiff and then discovered that Wales and England were playing a rugby match that day. The place was crowded with supporters. Thankfully, rugby supporters are friendly people and there was a pleasant atmosphere between them and the opposition. It did, however, make it difficult to find somewhere to eat, as everywhere was crowded.

We somehow made it through the day, and the concert was amazing! For those two hours, as I listened to Joan, I forgot about everything else and got into the music.

Trying to find the train back to Helen's cousin's flat in Bristol was a bit of a nightmare. Everyone was trying to get home, and the station was very crowded. After asking where to get our train, we were told, *"Go that way, but you will have to run as it is leaving in two minutes!"* (If you knew Helen and me, you would realize we really don't do the 'running thing,' but we had no choice. We ran like lions were chasing us!) We made it on time for the train's departure, totally out of breath and looking like we had run a marathon. The advantage was that a couple of younger men took pity on us two old women and gave us their seats. (Sorry, Helen…I know you are not as old as I, but neither are you that young either. LOL!)

By the time we arrived at her cousin's house, we were shattered but happy, as we both really enjoyed the concert. Her cousin wasn't home, but she left a note telling us to help ourselves to some food. All we wanted was coffee, which she had, but the only milk she had available was coconut milk. Yuck! Coffee and coconut milk would have done nothing for my taste buds, so I drank some water instead.

The next day, we took the train home. By then, my stress levels had dropped a bit, purely because I had gotten out of the village and done something I enjoyed. Plus, I laughed…a **LOT**. Although Helen is my P.A., she has a lovely sense of humor. Sometimes (many times, actually), I use laughter as a defensive mechanism, but genuine laughter is truly good for the soul.

Having Helen for six hours a week really helps me. Initially, when I got funding for a P.A., a mental health support worker and I interviewed a couple of people (it should have been three, but one of them didn't show up). The other one, quite frankly, terrified me when she listed all her paper qualifications and what she could do for me. It sounded like she would be controlling rather than allowing me choices. When Helen breezed in stating she had no paper qualifications because she didn't think they were worth the paper they were written on, I was blown away! She also said she had experience with people who had learning difficulties but knew nothing about DID. (She does now!) The things we do allow me to be out safely. Having DID and switching when out makes me feel vulnerable and confused. Too many times, when out alone, I get lost and don't know where I am. Helen always gives me feedback about who she has been talking to, which is truly helpful to me.

I know Suzie loves doing and seeing things she would not under normal circumstances. As a seven-year-old, she can't wander around on her own. She also negotiates between us all when it comes to buying clothes. I often wish I could see for myself as Helen explains the arguments between Suzie and Trish over colors. For example, when trying to buy a new winter jacket, Suzie wanted the pink one. Trish, however, said she wouldn't be seen dead in pink. Negotiations took place in the middle of the shop, and a compromise was reached: Trish could have the blue jacket, and Suzie could have something pink to wear under it.

Over the few years I have had Helen in my life, we have done various things. She helps with weekly menu-planning, pointers to maintain personal care (haircuts, dentist, optician, etc.), social outings, exercise by way of regular walks in the countryside, accessing courses, house maintenance, a safe person to talk to, and gives my overall week structure. In all of those activities, she provides safety, engagement, and understanding of my different personalities. She provides a social outlet away from the professional environment as an attempt to offer 'normalization' in what I find to be stressful situations. She gives me the space to practice techniques learned from therapy or Maike, too. For example, I am learning how to say 'no' to things I don't feel comfortable with. She encourages me to have social interactions in shops, during courses, etc., and helps to keep us safe during times of switching. We reflect on coping skills and she provides reassurance at times of flashbacks and triggering situations. Through and through, Helen is a genuine diamond in the rough.

CHAPTER TWENTY-FOUR

A Week in Respite

> *I seriously dislike people who are fascinated by my DID.*
> *They don't really care or understand*
> *Just see us as some kind of fascinating freak show.*
>
> *Dissociative Identity Disorder Devon*

Quotes Creator

Just before the concert, I had spent a week in my usual respite place. (My psychiatrist and Maike had always said that going into respite was better for me than being in a hospital.) I felt comfortable there, as it was only about 40 minutes from home in a lovely little town. The respite only had six bedrooms. I had been there several times before and knew the staff, who were easy to talk to. They knew Suzie and Trish, so they were both comfortable, too—even though Suzie's conversations revolved around food. She would arrive at the office door saying she was hungry, and someone would help her decide what she wanted. Because there was a wide variety of choices in the fridge, she found it difficult to choose, but with a staff member helping her to see all that was available, she could decide for herself as to what she wanted to eat.

If Trish was in the sitting room watching TV, a staff member would come and ask if we had eaten. They understood when Trish was around, the last thing she would be thinking of would be food. The whole subject of food is a trigger for Trish, so she avoids eating. She was made to eat things when she was younger that resulted in her not wanting anything whatsoever in her mouth. She also gets furious at Suzie sometimes because if Suzie is eating something (usually something unhealthy, such as chocolate) and then disappears for some reason, if Trish takes over and finds chocolate in her mouth, she can't wait to spit it out. Lots of times, if Trish annoys Suzie, she will deliberately get her back by eating chocolate and doing a disappearing act in hopes that Trish will show up and have to cope with it. Those two have a running war between them. There are times when Trish will go out for a drink in the evening, return home, and disappear. If Suzie then shows up, she literally bounces off the walls because, at the age of seven, she can't cope with alcohol.

We seem to have strayed away from the subject of respite. Let's return there now.

My first night in respite, I didn't sleep too well — which was unusual. Normally, when I am there, I feel safe enough to have a good night's rest. I suppose I was too stressed at the time to relax immediately. The next morning, as I was trying to figure out what I wanted for breakfast, one of the support workers said he wanted to talk to me about something but had chosen to let me rest first. He went on to tell me that the respite was closing at the end of the month due to financial difficulties and they had only recently been told themselves. (It is a testament to how caring they are in that their main concern was the clients who went to them for respite rather than on themselves about to lose their jobs.) For me, however, the timing could not have been worse.

Respite houses are few and far between in the area. My immediate concern was if I needed somewhere to go, then the subject of going into the hospital may arise. Throughout my life, I have never done well in hospitals. I believe if you are stressed out or upset, the *last* place you want to be is in a hospital. Perhaps that's not a fair assessment, though. Many people find them helpful and supportive. We don't. The longest we have stayed in one was for four days, and it felt more like 40. Plus, it seriously upsets Suzie to be in a big place, with only adults surrounding her.

CHAPTER TWENTY-FIVE

"Wait! WAIT!!!"

IF YOU SEE ME OUTSIDE
SOMEWHERE
YOU MAY THINK THERE IS
NOTHING WRONG.
ON THE SURFACE I LOOK OK.
(UNLESS I AM HAVING A PANIC
ATTACK)
UNDER THE MASK I AM FEELING
AFRAID AND INSECURE.
WORRIED THAT SOMEONE WILL
TAKE ADVANTAGE OF ME.
I INWARDLY JUMP AT SUDDEN
NOISES.
GET TRIGGERED MY CERTAIN
SMELLS
OR PEOPLE WHO EVEN VAGUELY
LOOK LIKE MY ABUSERS.
I FIND IT HARD TO KEEP UP WITH
CONVERSATIONS.
ON THE SURFACE I LOOK OK
UNDERNEATH I AM A MESS
DISSOCIATIVE IDENTITY DISORDER DEVON

Quotes Creator

During the first six months of 2019, it was essential for me to get out of the village because just being there reminded me too much of the rape. If the weather was nice on a Friday, Helen and I would go exploring. We would set off to go somewhere particular and end up somewhere completely different because we would get lost on the narrow back roads in the area. Still, we always ended up somewhere nice.

We visited the Donkey Sanctuary, which Suzie loved. We went to various beaches where we collected pebbles, walked by riverbanks, and explored museums and art galleries. We found villages we had never been to and explored around them. Those afternoons out were important to all of us.

Suzie showed Helen the farm we spent our first seven years on and, as she ate ice cream, told Helen stories of life on the farm. Helen later told me she did have a problem that day, as Suzie wanted to explore the farm and couldn't understand that a **Private/No Entry** sign included her. Suzie argued that since she lived there years ago, she had every right to climb over the gate!

Every time I am out with Helen, she seems to spend a lot of time saying, *"Wait!"* We are a nightmare when it comes to crossing roads. I have no idea what happens, other than I don't seem to be aware of oncoming traffic.

That is nothing new. In Scotland, my friend Mary encountered the problem, too. We would approach the edge of a road and, just as I was about to cross, I heard, *"Wait!"* One day, I got fed up and put my hands up like they were paws, stuck my tongue out, and panted like a dog. When we got to the other side of the road, I said, *"If you insist on saying 'wait' like you're talking to a dog, you really should buy some chocolate as a treat for obeying."* The best way to deal with my stupidity with crossing roads is to turn it into a joke.

Helen has not read my first book. She said she wanted to learn about me by being with me rather than reading about me. I think that was a good choice. If she is unsure of something, she will ask me if she coped with it in an okay way for me. She certainly knows how to deal with my flashbacks. I recall the time we were in a museum and I suddenly saw something that brought back horrible memories: a mask that triggered a memory of ritual abuse. Helen calmly suggested we move on into the next room, which had tapestries. She then coaxed me into concentrating on my breathing, talking mostly rubbish at me to get me to laugh. That's a skillset one cannot learn by solely reading a book.

CHAPTER TWENTY-SIX

I AM Breathing!!!

We were taught to believe

You are not good enough.
You will never amount to anything.
You are a waste of space.
You will do what you are told.
You will keep quiet about it
You belong to us.
You will never be able to break free.
You will be punished if you try to get away.
You are bad and it's all your fault.

But the TRUTH is
ALL THE ABOVE WERE LIES.

I am good enough and it wasn't my fault.

Dissociative Identity Disorder Devon

I remember months previously, I went to see my GP with a list of physical complaints. He said what I described were symptoms of fibromyalgia. He explained that because of my history of abuse, now that I was getting help, very often, the trauma would express itself in my body. Because I was so disconnected from my body in Scotland, that explanation was a new one on me. In Scotland, if I felt pain, I could dissociate myself from it. It seems that this was another change, and I found it challenging. I, as Pat, was not used to feeling pain or discomfort.

My therapist would ask me questions like, *"Where do you feel 'such and such' in your body?"* I wanted to say, **"I don't know!"** because it felt like a difficult question — but we stuck with it. Most often, I felt the feelings in my stomach because most of my emotions were those of fear. We went on to look at what happened in my body when I had certain feelings. If I got angry, my body would get tense and fired up. That physical feeling affected my concentration. In turn, that would make me want to fight, argue, shout, swear, and confront people. In truth, as I seldom get angry, that would have been Trish's response. When I got anxious (which I often did because I envisioned danger where there probably wasn't any), my body would get tense, shaky, hot, and sweaty. My breathing became shallow and rapid, and concentration goes out the window. The temptation is to avoid places and people because I'd rather run away and escape whatever the situation.

Too many times, I phoned Maike while in that state because my anxiety turned into a blind panic. She would simply tell me to breathe. Often, I felt like telling her, *"I AM breathing! Otherwise, I'd be dead!"* She remained consistent, though. *"Breathe, breathe, breathe..."* she would say until I was calm enough to talk with some sense.

Now, without Maike's guidance and soothing nature, it seems I can't stop the physical behaviors and reactions with ease. I can, however, look at them later. I get a sheet of paper and write down what thoughts or feelings I was having just before the reaction started. What did it feel like during the experience? What did I do to stop the mood and behavior? How did I feel afterward?

This year, I know things have been happening that I am not aware of (moreso than usual). For example, I will be sitting watching TV, and the next thing I know, I am dressed in my jeans and soaking wet from head to toe – indicating one of us has been outside wandering around in the rain. Since I don't have the taste of beer in my mouth, I know Trish hadn't made a trip to the pub. I can only assume someone has been wandering in the area of the railway tracks, which is a terrifying thought.

CHAPTER TWENTY-SEVEN

Chocolate Ice Cream and a Pie

Life with DID

Trying to get dressed this morning
and wondering who the hell
threw out my favourite jeans.

Dissociative Identity Disorder Devon

During the second half of 2019, I have been away from the village several times. We went to Wales to stay with Joy and Robert in August and November, and we went to Scotland in October to visit Morag and her family. Because Helen had been off due to illness, she owed me several hours of work and asked if I would like to go to the North Coast for a weekend. We worked out how many hours she would charge for the trip, and we found a flat in a lovely village. What we were looking for was something inexpensive, with two bedrooms, in a village, and with outside space where we could smoke. We decided not to talk about anything that had been happening. We just needed to get away so we could all enjoy ourselves doing whatever we wanted.

We went for walks along the coast path, looked around the shops in the village, and visited the one at the foot of the cliff. As always, when in a new place, I was completely disoriented, so Helen had to make sure we were always in sight of each other. When I switch, I tend to forget I have a phone on me. Trish was sitting in a pub one evening having a pint before we returned to the flat, and she said to Helen, *"I hope you know where the flat is because I have no idea."*

I think Helen was coping well with the switching until that Saturday afternoon. She had made a very nice breakfast before we went out for a walk, thinking that it would be enough until our evening meal, except for coffee and cake while we were out. Suzie had different ideas. While out, we had been looking around the shops (the small villages have lovely craft shops) and were sitting on a bench beside the harbor when suddenly, Suzie popped up but didn't say anything. Something wasn't right with her, but she wouldn't say what it was. Helen told her that once the cigarettes were finished, we would go and find Suzie an ice cream. That didn't solve the problem. Eventually, she just blurted out that she was hungry and needed more than ice cream. We made a trip to the baker, bought a pie, and everything was fine. Poor Helen. She kept apologizing because she hadn't thought about Suzie being hungry. On the other hand, Suzie was too embarrassed to tell her. After the chocolate ice cream and pie, she was fine again.

I think there is still a general problem with all of us when it comes to asking for what we need, but it is much better than it used to be.

CHAPTER TWENTY-EIGHT

Equine Therapy 101

*I am tired of people who say
Dissociative Identity Disorder
does not exist.*

That we have dangerous personalities inside

*That we are too complex to be accepted
into survivors groups cos we may upset
people if we switch*

*Most of us go out of our way to hide the switches.
We are not dangerous.
I have DID and 'we' exist
whether you believe in it or not.*

Dissociative Identity Disorder Devon

I had visited an Equine Therapist many months prior to seeing my psychiatrist (at the end of 2018) to have a discussion with her about how she worked. She took me to meet the horses, Tim and Fred, and, quite honestly, they were huge—about 17 hands (about six feet) high and 750 kilos (over 1,600 pounds) each. Suzie thought they were as big as dinosaurs, which is how they would appear to a seven-year-old. I had a lot of questions for the therapist, but the following were my main two concerns:

What would the horses do if I had a panic attack?

What would they do if I switched to another personality?

She explained that if I had a panic attack, the horses would be aware and would remove themselves to safety. If I switched, they would relate to whoever was present. She went on to discuss how she worked, and that what I did would be my choice.

While we were talking and she was showing me around, the horses wandered off into the barn. She asked me, *"Why did they do that?"* My immediate answer was that they didn't like me. (I still struggle with the fact that people like me, so I was projecting those insecurities onto what I thought about the horses' behavior.) She said, *"No, it had nothing to do with you. The horses realized we were in conversation, and they weren't included, so they went back into the shed to do their own thing."*

The therapist had worked in the equine field for many years. She was experienced and had knowledge of PTSD and

118

had attended courses about DID. Many who work in the NHS have not attended courses. I am led to believe that it is because of money. It is seen as a good use of NHS resources to send staff on courses about anxiety and depression, for example, but because there are so few people with DID, it is not seen as a good use of funds. In reality, there are more people with DID than they think. We are too often misdiagnosed or just ignored by professionals who do not believe in the condition. **DON'T GET ME STARTED ON THAT SUBJECT!** I have been there, done that and got the t-shirt too many times to prove it!

So, when my social worker finally got the funding (even though it was for just four sessions), I rang the therapist immediately. My four sessions were between mid-September and mid-October of 2019.

My first session was a bit of a disaster, but nevertheless, I learned much about the horses and me. The weather wasn't good, and the horses were being irritated by the flies. I, on the other hand, was aggravated by my nervousness. They were in the field and didn't come near me, but at the same time, I didn't want them near me. We then took them to the barn. I felt trapped and terrified, so the therapist put their halters on and tied them to the fence inside the shed. That still didn't calm me down, so she opened the barn door so that I didn't feel trapped, giving me a means of escape. Both horses showed their agitation by pawing at the ground with their hooves (do horses paw?). Apparently, horses can hear the heartbeat of a human from a distance away and were sensing my agitation.

The therapist and I got a couple of chairs and sat down to do some deep-breathing exercises. Soon enough, I got the panic under control. What were the horses doing once I had it under control? They had stopped being agitated and were calm. My first lesson was that horses pick up on the mood of the humans around them. Once I was calm, I was invited to touch them by getting as near to them as I felt comfortable with, though she chose to keep them tethered. I managed that task, and we talked all the time about what I felt — not just in my head but in my body as well. I felt calmer and it felt soothing to touch them, even though I wasn't getting that close. I was prepared to jump back if they made a sudden movement. However, I felt totally concentrated and focused on where I was. So, although I was disappointed with my first session, I didn't feel it had been a total waste and looked forward to the second one.

The second session went much differently. We had a short chat in her office before meeting the horses, and she had a diagram explaining the Window of Tolerance. Personally speaking, I spend very little time in that space, but having said that, sitting writing this book has placed me there. Maybe I should take up writing as a full-time occupation!

I have seen the Window of Tolerance diagram many times before. Actually, I have so many copies of it in different files, I could either paper my walls with them or make lots and lots of paper airplanes! However, for those of you who haven't seen it, I will provide the details here. The copy I have came from my therapist in 2017. It does not have a source printed on it.

****

When someone is in their Window of Tolerance, they feel calm, collected, and connected. They can:

➢ Think and feel at the same time.
➢ Feel empathy.
➢ Have present-moment awareness.
➢ Feel safe, open, and curious.
➢ Self-soothe.
➢ Regulate their emotional state.
➢ Have access to intuition and insight.
➢ Have an awareness of boundaries (their own and others).
➢ Are relaxed, calm, and alert.

But circumstances, stress, triggers, etc., can bounce someone out of their Window of Tolerance into a state of Hyperarousal. This is the fight or flight response, which means the person:

➢ Is overwhelmed emotionally.
➢ Is unsafe.
➢ Is impulsive.
➢ Is angry.
➢ Is defensive.
➢ Has racing thoughts.
➢ Is hypervigilant.
➢ Has tension and is shaking.
➢ Feels ungrounded.
➢ Has poor judgment.

They can also bounce the other way into the Hypoarousal Zone. This leads to feeling:

➢ Flat with no energy.
➢ Unable to think clearly.
➢ Numb.
➢ Disconnected with no feelings.
➢ Unable to defend themselves or say no.
➢ Disassociated.
➢ Shameful.
➢ Withdrawn or isolated.
➢ Hopeless.

****

Before the therapist and I enter the yard where the horses are kept, there are double metal gates where I take a minute to get grounded before going in. During my second session, I was to be working with Tim — the more nervous of the two. Usually, Fred has to do something first before Tim would do it, and the therapist thought it would be good for Tim if I worked with him on his own to improve his confidence. A nervous horse and nervous client didn't seem to be a good combination to me, but it worked out fabulously!

At the top end of the yard, there was a paddock which, because of the weather, was pretty muddy. It had obstacles in it like old tires, railway sleepers, barrels, and narrow gates. I felt comfortable enough to lead Tim up the yard toward the paddock. I can see it in my mind now: I led him up the yard while holding the reign in my right hand (my preference). To get into the paddock, Tim had to step over a six-inch wooden boundary. He just stopped as if to say, *"No way am I going to do that!"* The therapist suggested I find the right tone of voice to say, *"Come on,"* to him. It was important not to pull him, as it had to be his choice to step over the barrier.

That doesn't apply to just horses; it applies to me, too. Professionals especially have to find the right tone of voice and definitely not pull! Like a horse, I will dig in my heels, and they will not get me to do what they want. Talk to me gently, encourage me, and let me make the choices (unless, of course, my choices are putting me in danger). This stems from being shouted at by my abusers and told what to do.

Eventually, I found the correct tone, and off we went into the paddock. The therapist explained that Tim did not like narrow spaces, so she wanted me to get him to walk in between two barrels, through a narrow gate, take a sharp left, and return to her by going over the railway sleepers and through a narrow pathway. I found it disconcerting that she stayed outside the paddock, reminding me that Tim weighed 750 kilos and could slip...as could I. **Guess what?** *We did it and truly enjoyed ourselves!*

As we stood talking afterward (the therapist and me, not Tim and me—LOL!), she said I had a natural affinity with Tim and that to help him turn in the direction I wanted him to go, I used my shoulder. It was only as I was driving home that I had a 'EUREKA MOMENT.' I was mentally processing the session when I realized that before I went into the paddock, I moved to the other side of Tim, so I was holding the reign with my **LEFT** hand and using my left shoulder to encourage him to turn corners. It hit me like a ton of bricks that Suzie was there, as it is she who uses her left hand for many things. So, although I had been unaware at the time, it seemed that both Suzie and I were working together with Tim. It confirmed to me that my desire for Equine Therapy had not been misplaced. Plus, when I was with the horses, I was totally within my Window of Tolerance.

CHAPTER TWENTY-NINE

Joyce's Red Robin

> SOME SAY THAT HEALING IS GETTING BACK TO YOUR REAL SELF BEFORE THE ABUSE HAPPENED. I DON'T KNOW WHO MY REAL SELF IS SO HEALING FOR ME IS BECOMING SOMEONE NEW.
>
> DISSOCIATIVE IDENTITY DISORDER
> DEVON

A t this point in my writing, my mind has just digressed again. I needed a break for a cigarette and was smoking out my sitting room window.

A robin was sitting in the car park looking up at my window very calmly. Robins were Joyce's favorite bird and, when I see one, it always reminds me of her. I wonder if she's looking down on me, pleased that I am writing again.

I must say that this day is much better than the day after I was dragged off the train tracks when a robin was jumping around the car park like a possessed bird!

Joyce often told me years ago that seeing a robin was a sign that someone who had died had come to say, *"Hello!"*

CHAPTER THIRTY

Suzie Speaks Aloud

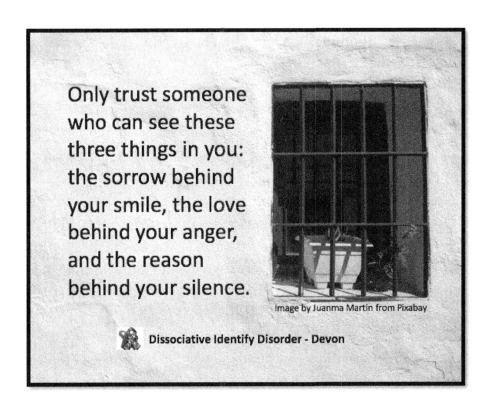

Only trust someone who can see these three things in you: the sorrow behind your smile, the love behind your anger, and the reason behind your silence.

Image by Juanma Martin from Pixabay

Dissociative Identify Disorder - Devon

When my Equine Therapy session #3 came, it had been raining heavily again, so working in the paddock would have been too dangerous (yes, it rains a **LOT** in this area). My therapist told me both horses were loose in the yard and asked if I was okay with that. Strangely enough, I was. At the therapist's request, I had brought my iPad with me for this visit, as she said she would take some photos of my time working with the horses so I could remember those moments. I thought that was a lovely touch.

I was given a stethoscope so I could listen to Tim's heartbeat. Suzie, however, was more interested in listening to the rumblings his stomach made! Due to his time in the yard, Tim's hooves were covered in mud, so we washed it off and put on the horse-equivalent of nail polish. As previously discussed, Suzie's left-hand preference made it evident when she was present. The therapist watched as we switched from right hand to left. With my right-handed nature, I cleaned the mud off the front hooves, and Suzie the rear (she is obviously braver than me). The same instance occurred when we cleaned the stones and dirt from underneath his hooves.

I then decided Tim's body needed to be brushed after the cleaning of his hooves. I tried out different brushes to see which one he liked. If he didn't favor one, he would turn his head away. When he took a liking to another, he would hold his head up, looking straight ahead. I could see he was relaxed. Brushing his lower front legs was a bit difficult, as I couldn't see what his head was doing. I believe it's safe to say he was okay because he didn't walk off (something he could have done at any point). Time and again, Suzie proved the braver one of us. She would brush closer to his rear than I would. I didn't much fancy possibly being kicked by his rear legs, though the therapist said that if he hit me with his head, that would hurt, too!

By this time, trust had been established between Tim and me, so I felt it okay to work with him while the therapist took pictures. At one point, Tim walked away from me and to the top of the yard. As usual, my thought was that I had done something wrong. When the therapist asked me why he walked away, I said, *"Probably because he is fed up with me."*

"Listen carefully," she instructed.

As I did, I heard a noise in the distance. Tim's instinctual response was to check to see if there was danger nearby. His sudden departure had nothing to do with me!

At the end of that session, I put Tim's coat on him. He had the patience of a saint, as I had it inside out, upside down, and every which way before I figured it all out. The front and rear straps were connected without a problem, but there were two straps underneath his body, which meant I had to stretch under him to grab hold of the longer strap. No way!!! It was then I got the shock of my life. As clear as a bell, I heard Suzie say, *"I am not scared. I can do that."* I almost had a heart attack! The only times I have **EVER** heard her was when she screamed *"NO!"* if any of us were near a railway track. (As I sit here writing, I realize now that although I have always described her voice as a scream, it was more of a scared plea — much like a 'no' that says, *"Please don't,"* in a frightened voice.)

In our conversation after the session, I was talking to the therapist about what happened because she had noticed all the way through the change of hand-use. We discussed why Suzie might have chosen then to speak. Perhaps it was because the therapist's property used to be a farm. Maybe it reminded Suzie of the farm when we were young, a time when she felt safe being with dad. I don't know the answer with any surety, but to **HEAR** her talk to *ME* for just a second was the most amazing experience!

CHAPTER THIRTY-ONE

Tim & Fred's Fun Time

Have you gone into a meeting with new professionals, been so stressed you switch like crazy and come out thinking well I hope to hell they knew what I was talking about cos I sure as hell don't

Dissociative Identity Disorder Devon

Quotes Creator

I approached the final Equine Therapy session with sadness. While I was sad, Trish was fussing about something (who knows what). As I stood in between the two gates, there was so much anger coming from her. (Oh. Wait. She just told me it was about a letter we had received that morning that seriously annoyed her.) I was concerned the horses wouldn't come near me because of the anger coming from her. Then, the strangest thing happened: Fred came up to the gate and stuck his head over to greet me. After stroking his head, he walked away to allow Tim to do the same.

Since it was my final session, I was given a choice on what to do. I chose the paddock. That time, I had a loose rope around Tim's neck. We made an obstacle course with all sorts of things, including hula hoops that he had never seen before, higher things for him to step over, and a narrow gateway that had an obstructing pole across it. *"This could be interesting,"* I thought. Again, I was totally within my Window of Tolerance, thinking about nothing except Tim, me, and the moment.

Walking around an obstacle course with barriers had as much to do with us as it had to do with Tim. We had lots of obstacles in our lives at that moment, and they made us as nervous as they made Tim. I took him around the course in the order I wanted to go. When we approached the narrow gate, I removed the pole so we could walk through.

After a while, the therapist asked if it was okay to let Fred come into the paddock so he could freely roam around. Well, it was my last session, so I thought, *"Why not live dangerously?!"* All went well until I led Tim towards the hula hoops. Fred decided he liked hula hoops, so he came over, took them into his mouth, and threw them in the air. I was prepared for Tim to freak out, but he didn't. We just walked past the mischievous Fred without a problem. All the while, the rope around Tim's neck was so loose, it was as if he was choosing to walk beside me. We could have stayed in that paddock for hours, enjoying the sense of joy with the relationship that had been built up over the space of four sessions!

Afterward, the therapist stated I had a real affinity with horses. She mentioned how, when I wanted Tim to walk through strange obstacles, I waited for a bit to let him look at where we were going. I hadn't been aware of that, but I guess that was coming from me. The lesson learned was that if I must do something new or deal with an obstacle in life, I need time to look at it before taking it on.

To really make my day, as I put on Tim's coat, Suzie told me I was a coward and that she would do the difficult straps again.

After the last session, I decided I had to go on the hunt for more money so that I could have more Equine Therapy sessions. It may sound strange, but I really miss Tim. But, as the therapist said, *"I don't think I have seen the last of you."* (I don't think she has either.) I still find it mind-blowing that Suzie spoke directly to me, that I was totally in the moment, and was working on my own obstacles (as well as Tim's). It also amazed me that I so easily trusted the therapist from the very beginning. The fact that I felt so "whole," especially in the last two sessions, hinted that we were all there. If those things could happen in four sessions, imagine what could happen with more! My hunt for more money continues. Because of my determination, I don't doubt I will find it!

CHAPTER THIRTY-TWO

Pat, Suzie, and Trish's Place of Beauty

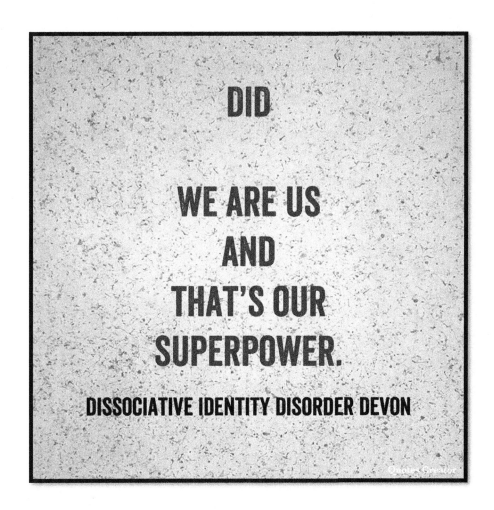

During my CAT therapy sessions, my therapist asked me to think of somewhere I would go if I could go anywhere. The following week, I sat down to think about it and was surprised because Suzie, Trish, **AND** I contributed to where that place would be. In the following session, I shared our thoughts with her, and she said it was a beautiful place—although I had to explain to her which personality had written what, as she had never seen our different styles of handwriting before. This is the scene we described:

Suzie is flying on a magic carpet with her little bear and lilac rabbit. She lands gently on the grass. There is a mountain behind and in front, with grass and a river in between. There is a cave built into the mountain. Inside the cave, there is a wood burner, and the floor has deep, thick fur. There is a soft bed in the corner with a multi-colored quilt. Windchimes and dreamcatchers blow with the wind. There are also coloring books and lots of crayons.

Trish said there is a fire pit outside and a gun so she could shoot rabbits (or whatever) and a fishing rod to catch fish. That is so they can eat...but she doesn't know who would cook. (Suzie said there would be a pixie who would cook and a unicorn that will come every day with chocolate and chocolate milk.)

I said that outside, I can see lots of trees and hear the birds singing. I could also hear the river roaring and see salmon jumping upstream. Brown bears are trying to catch the salmon, too. There are deer there with their babies. When I walk across the grass, I must be careful not to stand on the baby deer, as they are asleep in the hollows in the grass. There are golden eagles in the sky and red squirrels around, too. My old dog is there with me, and we sit together watching everything going on around us. The bears are friendly, and there is no one else around for miles. Were there other people present, my dog would protect me anyway.

Suzie said there are no insects anywhere, which is good because she hates insects.

Trish said that a drone flies in and drops down some tins of lager, which she keeps in the river so that they stay cool.

I found a hammock in the cave and hung it between two trees where I could listen to the sounds around or listen to music on my earphones.

Suzie said she could toast marshmallows on the fire pit just outside the cave and read fairy storybooks.

Trish said there is a quad bike, so she can go exploring and get a break from teddy bears and fairy storybooks. She would go to the top of the mountain with a couple of tins of beer to get some peace.

I said there are lots of bluebells among the trees. I will make a swing attached to a branch and wind some bluebells around the rope, so it is like a bluebell swing. I find a small, Indian-style canoe so that I can explore a bit further downstream. I take a picnic with me so that I can sit on the riverbank and consume it before going back to the cave. At night, I wrap up in an Indian-style blanket at the entrance, watch the sun go down, and then gaze up at the stars.

****

I found that piece of writing interesting. Three of us worked together to design a space where we all had things we enjoyed, along with our different places. However, at the time, I just thought it was an interesting story, not an achievable reality. Interestingly, Tracy, Heather, Cath and Anne did not contribute to the story.

CHAPTER THIRTY-THREE

"OUR" Inner Spaces

I don't feel the need to forgive my abusers.

I do feel the need to forgive myself for believing I deserved it, wasn't worthy, and unlovable.

Dissociative Identity Disorder Devon

Quotes Creator

Months down the line, I started thinking of "inner spaces." Had I started to develop the idea of an inner space where we all lived? I drew a picture of what I had written and began to expand on it, allowing space and time for all of us to make contributions. On paper, we were beginning to communicate what we needed in our space.

Suzie developed her cave and had all the things she liked in there. It became "her cave," although she was willing for others to see it. More fluffy toys were in there, more fairy storybooks, and a TV on which she could watch the films she liked. She had a fridge with her favorite foods, and paints and an easel so she could draw pictures. The pixie would leave her food at the entrance to the cave. It became her private space where she lived when she was not out in the world. She also had a door on the entrance to the cave that she could shut when she did not want to be disturbed. Her fire pit moved into the cave so that she could toast marshmallows. Her cave was full of color, with **LOTS** of pink, windchimes and dreamcatchers. She had pictures on the walls of unicorns and horses. She also had a rocking horse on which she could play and a toy farm with animals. Her bed was built into an alcove in the cave's wall with fluffy bedding and a multicolored blanket. Her teddy bears shared the bed with her. She had a rail for all her favorite clothes. (As I write this, I realize it is Suzie who is writing and sharing her space with me for the first time!)

My private space was mostly outside, among the trees with the river flowing through. (It changed from what I earlier described.) I had a cave to sleep in, too, but it was a small, functional one. It had the hammock inside, where I slept with my old dog to protect me. It had bookcases along one wall and lots of writing paper so that I could write stories. I also had art supplies. There was a computer in there and lots of music. My space also included the outside with the bears and eagles, but it was a contained space. The outside space had a wall around it so no one else could see or come inside. There was a door in the wall, but it remained shut unless I went out (I guess that meant when I go "out front" and live the outer life).

Trish had a cave, too, just a bit to the right of Suzie's and mine. It had a door, too, with a **"KEEP OUT"** sign in large letters. She still had the gun, but not for shooting rabbits. Instead, it was for threatening unwelcome visitors, potential intruders, and for keeping us all safe. She had a desk, computer, and books about how to make things, although she didn't have supplies in the cave to make anything. The cave had a small fridge, and the only thing in it was her cans of beer. She lived with a black panther. She had some purple pictures on the walls and a few model motorbikes. Apart from that, it was quite spartan. That is because she spent all her life being the protector of Pat and Suzie and has not worked out yet what she really enjoys. (This description of her cave has just been described and shared with me for the first time.)

Behind Trish's cave were another four caves where Tracy, Heather, Anne, and Cath lived. They were situated in the dark where the sun does not reach — small caves with large, black doors. I don't know what they have inside their caves, and, at the moment, they do not seem willing to write anything about them. I sometimes hear crying from that direction but don't know from which cave the sound comes. Is it one cave or several?

Perhaps some of the cries I can hear are coming from Trish. She has changed so much in the last two years, based on the feedback I get from Helen, Maike, and Joy. She is not as angry as she used to be. She seems to be uncertain, confused, and upset.

Presently, there is no common area where we all meet up. Hopefully, that will evolve. A lot has changed since we first wrote the story to our therapist, so I am sure it will evolve even more over time. Wouldn't it be great to have a communal space where we could meet up and talk to each other? If I get to the point of being co-conscious, no doubt the communal space will happen.

CHAPTER THIRTY-FOUR

Inner Spaces: DID Friends' Contributions

DOING THERAPY AS SOMEONE
WITH DID IS HARD.
WE NEVER KNOW WHO IS
GOING TO GO.
BUT IT'S IMPORTANT WE ALL
GET
TO SPEAK OUR OWN THOUGHTS.
NO PARTS OF US SHOULD BE
IGNORED.
NO MATTER HOW CONFUSING IT
GETS FOR THE THERAPIST.

DISSOCIATIVE IDENTITY DISORDER DEVON

Quotes Creator

While I was thinking about inner spaces, I wondered if that development was crazy or if others with DID had the same. So, I started talking and asking questions of others with the condition. I learned that some had inner spaces; others didn't. Again, this seems to confirm we are all different in how we experience ourselves. Having inner spaces does not make us better or worse than those who don't. They are not a prerequisite to healing. Some with inner spaces developed them by themselves, some were created by their alters, and some were helped by therapists. Some of my DID friends gave me permission to share their inner spaces, so I do so without mentioning their names. In doing this, I hope to provide you with an idea of how those spaces differ from person to person.

Each of the following describes several different spaces:

➢ They live in a castle with two others who sort of live there, too. At the center is a huge fountain, apartments, and bookshops that surround it, and lots of them who live there are roommates. Then, there is a little area with a cottage where the gatekeeper lives. Another lives in the haunted hills, which is sort of based on where we lived during the younger years. It's a kind of big and small place at the same time. Most of them live in the middle where the fountain is and, when there is a staff meeting of sorts, then everyone goes to the castle.

➢ We meet in the kitchen around a cozy fire.

➢ One male lives in my garden, one lives in one of my vehicles, one sleeps in a long glass case that's magical-looking, and one hides in the shadows my host creates —

144

almost hiding behind the host, peeking out but never speaking…just watching.

> Mine is centered around a very large, warm, and dusty library. There are two open floors of books and wooden filing shelves with a railing on the top to prevent falling. On the bottom floor in the middle of the room is a large, round table with a chair for everyone inside. There is also a bedroom for each of my people. Openings for their doors rest between the bookshelves. One of those doors, however, leads to the outside and the front. There is a small porch outside the front door and, beyond that, the grass which is our 'fronting.' Once you step into the grass, you are either fronting or co-conscious. The way we look at it is that if they are in their bedroom, they don't know what is going on outside of their rooms or the body. If they are at the table or in the library, they can hear what is going on, but not see. If they are on the porch, they can see and hear, but they are not fronting. That is our systems' workings.

> Most of mine live in their own scenarios from the past that created them. Therefore, if I dream, it can be utterly lifelike and terrifying. It is chaos when they decide to clean the house and invade each other's space. Sometimes, older alters will bring some sense to the younger alters' way of reaction, although not always in time for negative occasions. Group discussions can be quite lively. There is, however, a dark side. Some of my teen alters have morphed into darker versions, living in places in me which I would never have believed. My system is very private and will never live anywhere out of earshot of each other.

➢ I don't know where mine are or how they live. They are just with me, watching and being vigilant. I just sense them as being together and working as a team in me.

➢ I have a long hallway now. It is constantly under construction but not noisy, kind of like a hallway in a hotel. Each head mate has their own room but do not have to stay in it. As alters I have not met yet, when they present themselves, another room is added. For parts I feel but cannot find (or find their names yet), it is like they are whispers in the walls. My headspace started as the house I lived in as a kid and has morphed over the years to this giant hallway now.

➢ My alters view each other as a very close-knit family, so we all 'live' in a three-bedroom home. Each has their own respective rooms. I asked two of them to draw what their rooms look like, and the differences really shocked me.

➢ There is a porch, and properly inside, there is a kind of sitting room, I guess. There is nothing to sit on properly, but there is a low, round table in the middle of the room. There are doors leading out of this room — one for each of us — and, if you are looking from the porch, you can't see all of them at once. The doors move sometimes but stay equidistant, and only the person who the room is 'for' can enter their door. As far as I know, they all go to different places. We can keep things in there that we don't want the others to see, so I guess the doors are like a mental image of the dissociative barriers between us. Anyway, you can't see or feel what is behind the doors, so our rooms are also where we stay when we are dormant.

> ➢ There is a communal 'living room' with a space for entertainment for them, a computer desk, and a decent kitchen for them to use where everyone usually hangs out. It's like a giant circle, but then it branches out into hallways with doors for everyone's rooms. If anyone isn't available for whatever reason or they go dormant, they lock their door. There is also an office that is basically the 'control room' where whoever is fronting goes. So, when someone is 'front locked,' they are locked into that room. Everyone's room is more than just a reflection of their personality. Occasionally, it's an entire world of their own.

It becomes clear from the above descriptions that everyone's inner spaces look different. There is a common denominator: the mention of different rooms where the different personalities live. It is also apparent that we all use **different** terminology to relay a *similar* message.

CHAPTER THIRTY-FIVE

Christmas in 'The Village'

More downsides of DID

Dissociative identity disorder devon

Who threw out my favourite jeans?

Who used my credit card?

Who bought that horrid sweater?

Who went out and came home with bruises?

Who spoke to my therapist?

Who threw out the food in the fridge?

Who got drunk and left me with the hangover?

Who? Where? When?

Although I was making progress with the use of colored pens and developing our inner spaces, I realize I am still struggling with feelings of shame and worthlessness. Just when I was beginning to work through those feelings, the rape happened and brought it all back. And because of the lack of therapeutic input, I am struggling to deal with it. I am also aware that I start a lot of my sentences with the word 'sorry.' On a logical level, I know I have nothing to be sorry about, but it feels like I am almost apologizing for my existence. I think, too, that always saying 'sorry' stems from our childhood when our dad always told us just to "keep the peace." No child should be instructed in that way. No child should be put under that kind of pressure. Keeping the peace meant that my needs were always denied.

Trish is having problems, too, because she feels sorry for not being able to protect us in the same way she used to. Cath, Anne, Tracy, and Heather are definitely sorry they exist. They feel guilty because they blame themselves for being the ones immersed in the ritual setting. They blame themselves because of the effect it had on Suzie and me in particular. They struggle with trying to accept that none of it was their fault. In many ways, they want to return to Scotland. Life in the ritual setting was one they understood. They likely won't understand this life of being free. I haven't been much help to them either by focusing my hatred on them.

Last year, I made a few trips to the farm shop where Suzie was raised. I often found myself sitting on a bench outside the shop, thinking, *"What if? What if we hadn't been taken to Scotland? What kind of life would we have had? Being with my dad's family would have been a life of being accepted and loved. Would I have become the lawyer I feel would have been my direction? Or are my thoughts of being a lawyer influenced by the life I had in Scotland?"* Surely, my life would have been better had we not gone to Scotland...or is that just me dreaming? There is a chance I would have ended up married and in an abusive marriage or something similar. My assumption is that life would have been better, but perhaps it wouldn't have been. Letting my mind dwell on the 'what ifs' isn't healthy. I must live in the present and find the answers on how to make a life now.

In the last six months of 2019, I became more sociable in the complex of properties where I live. I always kept to myself and was seldom seen, except for trips to the communal laundry. I never attended the weekly coffee mornings with the other property owners. About six months ago, a new manager was appointed who had ideas for having activities in the lounge. I began to go to some of them, and people said it was good to see me getting involved. I discovered, though, that when there is a group of people there, I mostly stayed quiet because being in groups still makes me dissociate rapidly, making keeping up with conversations difficult. I certainly couldn't play bingo. Not only do I dislike the game, but rapid switching meant I couldn't keep up with the numbers called. The manager suggested I sit beside her, and she offered to watch my card. No way! People would notice and wonder why, as one of the youngest residents, I couldn't do it for myself.

I was happier if I just went to the lounge when two or three people were there. Then, I could keep up with conversations. But even then, those conversations would be upsetting when the residents talked about their families and the lives they lived when they were younger. Their stories were interesting but highlighted the fact that I don't have children or grandchildren and didn't have the "ordinary" lives they had. Gradually, I found out that everyone had sadness in their lives, and I discovered I could react to them with empathy. My biggest fear, though, was that I would openly switch in front of them.

For someone who wants to raise awareness of DID, it seems that in public situations, I want to cover it up. Perhaps I still am uncomfortable with 'us' being seen.

The manager (who I found out had read my first book before taking on the job) organized a Christmas party. That caused an internal argument. Suzie wanted to go because there would be food, a big Christmas tree, Christmas music, and games. Trish could think of nothing worse. It made me nervous. So, a compromise was made: Trish left a note for Suzie saying, *"Don't open your mouth,"* and another saying that both Suzie and I could stay until 5:30. That's when the pub opened, and she could do something she wanted. It kind of backfired on her, though, because when she walked into the pub with Christmas music playing and decorations all around, she didn't stay there long.

On Christmas Eve, the village's carol singers came to the lounge. They sang in different places in the village before coming to our building. The manager and her husband came for the carols and brought their two dogs. One is named

Ted/Teddy—a little rescue dog that had been poorly treated until it went to live with them. He was really nervous and didn't like men, so he came in his little anxiety bag. He felt comfortable in there with only his head popping out from the bag that was draped across the manager's shoulder. Trish (again) could think of nothing worse, but she knew about the dog coming, so there was another compromise made: a note was left for Suzie that said, *"Keep your mouth zipped,"* and another saying, *"At the end of the last carol, I am going to the pub, not staying for coffee."* Well, the inevitable happened. Suzie decided she wanted to have the dog over her shoulder and laughed lots because Ted's head would suddenly disappear into the bag and then pop out again like a jack-in-the-box. She found it so funny! I found it seriously worrying. Was she talking as well as laughing? It seems she didn't. Thank goodness. When the last carol ended, Trish immediately went to the pub. That was another short visit, as they had a brass band playing carols. Trish felt there was no way of avoiding what she called "Christmas rubbish." Still, it seemed there was communication going on, even though Trish could have worded her notes to Suzie in a more polite way. Telling her to 'zip it' wasn't exactly friendly.

Christmas day itself was a bit of a first. In conversation with Helen, it was decided that Suzie could have the day, based on the fact that none of the rest of us liked the day. Suzie was the one who opened the presents and had the tree lights on all day. We showed up at different points, but mostly, it belonged to her. With Helen, Suzie bought lots of things she liked to eat that didn't require cooking. At most, some things needed microwaving. What she didn't tell even Helen was that on our previous online shopping excursion, she had ordered from a turkey joint that cooked in a foil package in the oven. She also had ordered frozen roasted potatoes, frozen Brussel sprouts, and gravy granules. Later in the day, I really felt sorry for Suzie. She doesn't use the oven for fear of us switching, burning things, or setting the house on fire. I am unhappy with ovens for the same reason. In the past, we have burnt several pans by merely trying to boil an egg. The person who wants the egg dissociates, and no one else realizes the egg is boiling.

In the evening, I discovered lots of notes on the footstool: the time the turkey went in, the time the roasted potatoes went in, and when to boil the Brussel sprouts – plus notes for when they all came out and a note that said the turkey had to rest for ten minutes because it was "tired." That was followed by a note that said she (Suzie) was very tired, too. She even took a photo of it all on the plate. There must have been cooperation for those two or so hours because we didn't switch. It was left to Suzie to do it. While it may seem mean to leave a seven-year-old to handle such things on her own, it was the best way. If I had taken over, I would have done something wrong, as I can't handle too many things happening at once. If Trish had taken over, she would have removed everything from the oven and thrown it in the trash in pure frustration. So, thanks to Suzie for the Christmas lunch, even though I didn't taste any of it. She cooked it, so she deserved to eat it! Sadly, she hasn't made anything since…not that I know of, anyway. Perhaps it was too difficult for her and she has reverted to the occasional ready-meal in the microwave.

CHAPTER THIRTY-SIX

There's HOPE for "US" Yet!

Today is January 1, 2020. The final day of 2019 ended on a positive note. I had a review with a locum psychiatrist I had never met before. Usually, I am not okay with the first meeting with a professional, but that one put me at ease. I think what surprised me was that he had a really good understanding of DID and asked relevant questions.

We were talking about how I found it frustrating that Suzie would go onto the internet and buy things she liked on sites that had my debit card stored. All she had to do was push the 'Buy Now' button. He asked, *"Do you send the things back or keep them?"* I replied that I kept them. Because I did, he said that there was some form of cooperation between us.

I remember being angry with Suzie because she recently bought three hoodies. It doesn't seem to matter to her how much money is in the bank! When I thought about it last night, I realized she purchased three because she was thinking of us all. She had a pink one for herself, a blue one for me, and a green one for her twin Tracy. Interestingly, the green one has not been worn, but Tracy tends not to be out in public. Suzie didn't buy one for Trish, as Trish already has a purple one. So, I shouldn't really have been angry at her. Instead, I should've been pleased that she was thinking of some of us…even though she was trying to dress us all in hoodies! Hoodies are fine, though. None of us dress in a particularly feminine way. We don't wear low-cut tops, short sleeves, or skirts. I find short sleeves embarrassing because of the scars of my wrist. Plus, I don't like my body, so I prefer to keep it hidden (mostly from myself).

The psychiatrist and I also spoke about driving. Trish and I are the only ones who drive, and, in our lifetime, we have never had an accident or speeding ticket. I told him about the day Suzie had been talking to my therapist at the end of a session. The therapist, who I called "Cat Woman" (Cognitive Analytical Therapist) in my previous book, said that Suzie should not leave because the car was in the car park and she couldn't drive. She told Cat Woman it was okay because someone would show up by the time she reached the car. I think the therapist didn't quite understand that.

Well, the locum psychiatrist completely understood and said it was another sign of cooperation between us.

Those two examples were things I had never thought of as cooperation before. That "knowing" increased my hope that things were changing. The only thing I wasn't thrilled with was that he was recognizing the personal danger I was in by living on my own, especially when one of the other four personalities were going out. I had no idea where they were going, but my gut instinct tells me they are spending too much time in the vicinity of train tracks. Because we switch numerous times in a day, I could see from where his concern came.

He asked if I had ever thought of having a relationship with a man and living with him. **No way!** I have never had a non-abusive relationship with a man before and can't see it happening at this late stage in my life. Plus, it would take a special kind of man to live with someone with DID. While I know many people who are living with DID in happy relationships, I just don't see it happening for us. The psychiatrist then suggested I have a flatmate because if I had someone living with me, I would feel safer and could function better. He went on to say my mental health would improve if I were not afraid of things going wrong in the house or one of my personalities going for walks to who knows where. I think when you have DID and are not co-conscious, you can inadvertently find yourself in dangerous situations. That idea wouldn't work right now because I have a one-bedroom house. He then said he would talk to my social worker because in addition to those reasons, living in my house reminds me of the rape, and being in the village has me afraid of bumping into that guy at some point.

I came out of that appointment with some hope, though in the back of my mind was the comment he made that if the switching got too chaotic, perhaps a short time in a hospital would help—not for treatment, but as a calming measure. At that point, Trish popped up to tell him my original psychiatrist said respite was better, as putting a seven-year-old into a hospital would not be helpful. Trish's opinion of hospitals is worse than mine. As mentioned, the longest I have been in one is four days, and it was four days from **HELL**! I think the stress of being there made us switch **MORE**, not less. It was during that stay that a doctor asked if we would be willing to talk to some student doctors about DID. I would have said yes had it been now, but back then, I thought—or rather Trish thought— that we were not a freak show. It is only since moving to where I am now that Trish has decided psychiatrists are actually human and not the enemy. Most of her change of opinion is because the psychiatrists here relate to us as people and accept DID.

CHAPTER THIRTY-SEVEN

If I Had One Wish...

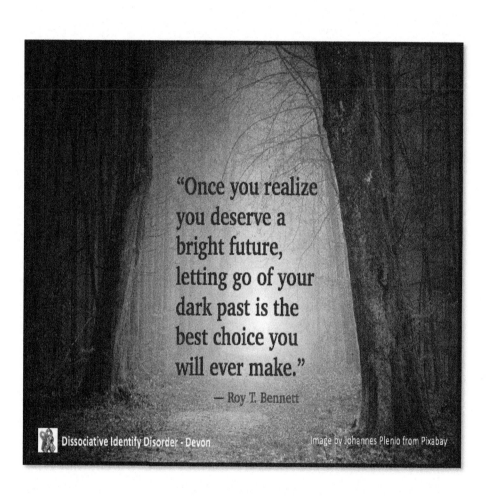

"Once you realize you deserve a bright future, letting go of your dark past is the best choice you will ever make."

— Roy T. Bennett

Dissociative Identify Disorder - Devon

Image by Johannes Plenio from Pixabay

It is now January 5, 2020. As I look back over the last year, I wonder, *"What was **THAT** all about?"* It seems it was a tumultuous year on many levels; natural disasters, political chaos, and, from what I have read, people with mental health problems found it chaotic, too. In the U.K., the government promised lifelong care for abuse survivors and more funding for NHS mental health services. In reality, it seems to have gone in the opposite direction: *LESS* funding for care packages, staff shortages, and longer waiting lists. So many are being left on their own to cope, unless they can afford to pay for a private therapist. Many volunteer services that gave support to mental health clients have either shut down or have serious financial difficulties. Those things are not just happening in the U.K., but worldwide. People are being left to fend for themselves. It should be no wonder why suicide rates are on the rise. Plus, as I expressed before, the number of sexual assault cases that make it to court is dropping, although the level of cases being reported is rising. What does that say about our society when victims are unable to get justice for the crimes committed against them?

Where am I as I enter this new year? It's evident to me that I am more traumatized than I was 18 months ago:

- ➢ The loss of Maike after three years.
- ➢ The loss of her replacement after three months.
- ➢ The wait for another new one has been destabilizing, to say the least.
- ➢ No permanent psychiatrist and not knowing which direction any new therapy may go causes me distress.
- ➢ Not to mention the train incident and rape.

All these changes have affected us all. Suzie is not as happy as she was and doesn't feel safe when she finds herself alone in the flat, as there is no one she can talk to. Yes, she rang SPA once but feels afraid to do it again in case she gets someone who doesn't understand. Trish sometimes feels like telling mental health services to go to Hell but deep down, she realizes that would not be a good move. I phone SPA, attempting to help keep myself going because just talking to them helps me to stay grounded. As for Heather, Tracy, Cath, and Anne, they have no one because they can't talk to a stranger at the other end of the phone. Plus, they wouldn't know what to say.

Although I feel alone in many ways, I remember that the people who are no longer around, like Joyce and Maike, are, in fact, still with me. My first book explained how much certain people helped and taught me things. Some of those people may have gone, but they are still inside me. What they taught me is still there, and I can pull on that knowledge.

If I had one wish, I would sit for an hour on a bench and speak with Joyce—face-to-face with a giant bear hug. I would love that! It may sound weird, but I so miss getting safe hugs. So does Suzie. Trish does, too, but she wouldn't admit to that. After so much touch that was abusive, being held and comforted in a safe way feels so healing. Everyone needs to experience safe touch. In the last six months, that has been missing from our lives. I can't really explain what that feels like. The closest I can come is relating it to sensory deprivation.

I remember talking to a 'duty worker' a few months back who suggested I calm myself down by hugging myself. Her intentions were good but at that point, I wasn't liking myself at all, so I couldn't self-soothe in that way. Trish can walk into the pub and get hugs from people she knows, but they are not the hugs we need. Those are polite 'hello' hugs without the "I genuinely care" feeling. Perhaps I am being too judgmental. Scotland was not a "hugging society," but England tends to be. In my local pub, men will give each other a greeting hug. In Scotland, if men did that to other men in a pub, it would probably start a fight or, at the very least, rumors about their sexuality. How can we live in the same country with different ideas on what is acceptable?

Helen hugs us sometimes when she comes to pick us up, but they are not quite the same. (Sorry, Helen. You are physically real thin, and it doesn't feel like a bear hug.) I do appreciate her thoughtfulness, though. Because I am no longer dog-sitting for my cousin, I miss the physical contact and soothing effects of stroking a dog. I miss working with the horses for the same reason. Thank goodness my respite place has lots of animals. When I visit, I can't wait to have dogs and cats around me. Being in their presence is so soothing and comforting—and Joy and Robert give **GREAT** bear hugs when I arrive!

CHAPTER THIRTY-EIGHT

"WE" Speak to Each Other

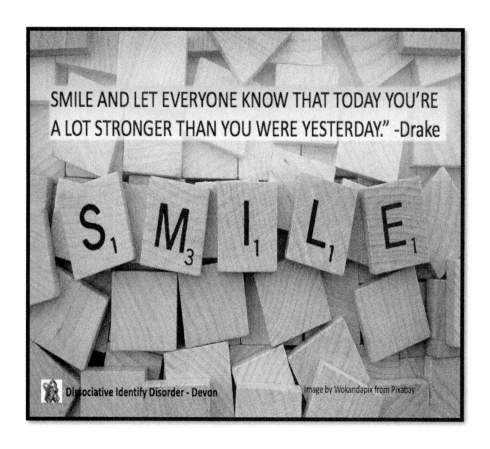

A couple of months ago, a professional stated to me that even though Suzie was only seven years old, she was actually older than any of us because she has been around the longest. That was a bit of a revelation to me because it's true. I still don't know where I fit into things. Professionals say I am the 'core personality,' but my memories do not go back as far as Suzie's. As I don't understand the technicalities of 'splitting,' I don't know if I existed before Suzie. Did I exist in the hospital as me for the first ten days before I was adopted? Was adoption and finding myself with an uncaring mother the first trauma that caused me to disappear and for Suzie to come into being? At this point, I do not know the answers to those questions.

My friend Sara believes Suzie is the core personality. Maybe the answers don't really matter in the greater scheme of things. One thing I do know for sure is that Suzie is the strongest and the one who has fought to keep us alive when we all want to give up. For that, I am grateful.

At the moment, my self-esteem is at a low point, which is understandable. I am struggling with both insults and compliments. In the past, I was used to being insulted verbally and told negative things about myself. I believed those insults, and, in a sense, I wasn't troubled by them because I believed the horrible things my mother's family said about me. During this last year, I have found that if anyone insults me and says I am not good in any way, I get upset. That's a new feeling for me. On the other hand, I find compliments difficult to handle because I don't like them either and don't know how to react. I have heard others receive a compliment, and they respond by saying *"Thank you"* or similar words. I suppose I just don't know how to accept compliments.

When I published my first book and read some of the positive reviews (some of which are shared at the start of this book), I didn't know what to do with that in my mind. I suppose I jokingly asked myself if they had written a good review of the correct book? I have met up with a couple of people in the village who have read that book and known it was me who wrote it. One person told me they thought I was the strongest person they had ever met (they obviously need to meet more people). I don't think I am strong, even though somewhere, I must be because I have made it this far. Sometimes, a person on Facebook will say I am "amazing." Frankly, I don't know what to do with that one. I am no more amazing than anyone else who has gone through abuse of any kind. Helen gives me compliments, but I don't know what to do with them either, except make a face which implies I don't believe her. There are times when she will come to pick me up and say I look nice. That one always gets to me, as I can't see anything nice about me at all. Even if I wear a new outfit or have my hair done, I can't see that either makes me "look nice." I know that if I buy something new, it takes me ages to actually wear it. The reason why that is, I have absolutely no idea — unless it is that wearing something for the first time makes me feel uncomfortable. I have a habit of sticking to wearing the same things. Doing so for several days at a time is partly due to a lack of interest in my appearance and partly as a coping technique. If I leave the previous day's clothes lying beside the bed, I just put them on. Well, that is if it is me that gets dressed.

We still have a problem if we are switching rapidly in the mornings. Some mornings, Suzie awakens and goes for something pink. I can live with that, but Trish can't, so another top goes on. Then, Suzie takes it off and replaces it with the pink one. That battle goes on until the bed is covered with discarded clothes, and I start getting frustrated. I have tried to partially solve the problem by buying jumpers with stripes or ones with mixed colors in them with the hope that I am not left cleaning up behind Suzie and Trish after they just dump things on the bed.

I also know that things have gone missing from the flat. For example, I have lost a whole pile of CDs. One day, they were there; the next, they disappeared. I used to collect bookmarks, but recently, when I went to find one for a new book, they had disappeared, too. I hunted high and low and only managed to find about four of them, whereas there used to be about 50 in my collection. Clothes disappear, and new garments appear. The other day, I was looking for a book I knew I had but couldn't find it in the bookcase. As I really wanted to read it, I was getting stressed and frustrated, blaming Trish for throwing it out. I mentioned it to Helen when she came, so she had a look and found it. In that instance, it was a case of me rapidly switching because I was stressed and quite simply couldn't see the book.

I am becoming increasingly annoyed by phrases like, *"It's all in the past," "You should just forget about it," "Why can't you just move on," "Everything happens for a reason," "What doesn't kill you makes you stronger,"* etc., etc. I don't think the trauma ever really leaves us. We just learn ways to cope with it better.

165

For me, being traumatized is not so much about me being stuck in the past as it is about not being able to be fully present in the moment, except on occasion. I can't decide that I am not going to have flashbacks, triggers, nightmares, or body memories. Yes, I can learn ways to deal with them, but I am still having them. Neither can I decide one morning that I will awaken and no longer have DID. Nice though, that would be!

Recovery takes years, and, in many ways, I am only truly about three to four years into my recovery. Yes, I had help in Scotland from fantastic people, but it has only been during my time in England that I started getting the help and support I need. Being away from the situation in Scotland has meant I can do the work I need to do without the constant fear of looking over my shoulder every day. I know that many people with DID are getting no support and having to deal with it on their own. I have nothing but admiration for them. What we really need are trauma-informed therapists with knowledge of DID. Unfortunately, there seems to be a lack of those professionals.

From my viewpoint, it would be good if we could 'interview' a therapist to see if we can work with them. In the NHS, we are allocated a therapist (if we are lucky) for the standard 40 sessions. In no way can we recover in 40 sessions. I have heard of therapists who dig around in memories too quickly and end up leaving their clients in a worse state than when they started. Memories are brought to the surface, and there is not enough time to deal with them. Or people are given a therapist who does not have the necessary experience, and the client makes no progress. We cannot open up too much too quickly. We need time, safety, and containment as we face horrendous memories.

What needs to be recognized is that if we have a memory from another personality, that memory does not feel like it is in the past. It is new to us and, therefore, the memory is in the 'NOW,' which is why getting a new memory sends us into shock. What also needs to be acknowledged by therapists is that all our personalities are at different stages in their recovery. For example, Heather, Cath, Tracy, and Anne are at the very beginning. As such, a therapist needs to work with them where they are. Just because I trust a therapist doesn't mean we all do. We all have different levels of trust. If, for example, a therapist breaks the shaky trust of Cath or Anne, there is the possibility they will sabotage the whole therapy process.

For me personally, I need the professionals who work with me to recognize that we all need the time to build trust. I need honesty, integrity, and authentic compassion. Also noteworthy is that they treat all my personalities with non-judgmental, unconditional positive regard. Believe me when I say that we can see through a non-caring professional a mile away — the ones who, for example, quote from books and are unwilling to move from what they have read or the ones who keep giving us sheets listing distraction techniques. Yes, they are useful in certain situations but personally, if I use distraction techniques every time, I panic or get stressed because I am not looking at the reason I panicked in the first place. I need to feel the feelings and try to work my way through them. It's the same with medication. I don't like medicines that dull my thinking processes. Yes, they may make me feel better in one way, but I need to think. The medications I am on take the edge off but still allow me to think and reason.

I believe that when dealing with DID clients, professionals must be willing to think outside the box. Just because a textbook refers to 'alters' does not mean that all their clients are happy with that word. I don't think there are two people with DID who present in the same way or use the same words to refer to themselves. We don't fit in the same boxes. If we are all different, we need professionals to try to understand our differences and realize the same approach for one DID client will not necessarily work for another. That may be asking a lot of a professional, but it is asking a lot of us if we get landed with people who are not willing to learn and treat us as human beings whose 'systems' are unique to them. The last thing we need is to be traumatized by therapists who think they are right and have all the answers. Please just give us some credit that we have an understanding of ourselves, no matter that sometimes that understanding is limited. Don't force the idea of integration if that is not what we want. Accept that some of us wish to be co-conscious instead.

Speaking of co-consciousness...

I have always said I want that. It may sound foolish, but it was only in the last months of 2019 when I realized that co-consciousness wouldn't be possible if we related to each other in the way we do.

I intensely dislike Anne and Cath. I blame them for being immersed in ritual abuse. I know they were involved in having to abuse or punish others who got out of line. I think they should be locked up and have the key thrown away. I can hear on the news that someone has been sent to prison for sexually assaulting someone and think, *"You two should not be walking around the world free, trying to recover enough so that you have a life."* I don't care how many professionals have tried to explain to me they didn't have a choice because they were brainwashed and totally controlled…that they were similar to child soldiers in other countries who had a gun put in their hands and told to kill the enemy and, if they didn't, they themselves would be shot. While I could sympathize with child soldiers, I cannot with Cath and Anne because they are a part of me. My intense dislike for them just won't shift.

I know now that Cath and Anne feel the same way about themselves. They live with intense, overwhelming guilt, and that's probably why they live in caves in the dark with such big doors. On an emotional level, it makes me feel sick to my stomach. Even writing about it raises so many emotions for me. I need to take a break to try and ground myself away from the thought that they don't deserve to live and, by implication, neither do I.

I kind of feel sorry for Heather because she was just a child who didn't deserve the pain she received. But because I always refer to Heather, Tracy, Anne, and Cath in the same breath, I am not too emotionally happy with her either. The same goes for Tracy. I think that just because they lived in a world of ritual abuse, I dislike them as a group.

What do I feel about Trish? I used to hate the fact that she was always angry. Anger terrifies me. I disliked the fact that her coping mechanism was to go for a couple of drinks. I disliked that she would fall out with people. I didn't like that she used to refer to Suzie as 'the little creeplet' and that she found her an embarrassment. Why didn't she find the other four to be an embarrassment? Suzie hadn't done anything wrong. In fact, all the wrong was done **TO** her. As such, I saw (and maybe still see) Trish as being heartless. I dislike her because she was the one who went to the train tracks. I know it was her because she was the only one who could be in the outside world and take the bus to get there. It certainly wasn't me who went there, and it **definitely** wasn't Suzie. I dislike that she calls herself our protector but, in a lot of ways, didn't protect. I dislike her because, ultimately, it was her decision to get everyone's agreement to get out of the cult. Why didn't she do that earlier?

What about Suzie? She is the one I feel okay about. I do worry that she will talk in inappropriate settings. Still, I like what she stands for. I love that she can laugh and have fun and that she wants to live and be happy. I like thinking that she enjoys watching Paddington films, eating ice cream, and playing with animals. I especially like that she is the only one I have actually heard speak a sentence directly to me. I like that she is brave—brave enough to cook Christmas lunch, brave enough to stop us (mostly) from going to the train tracks, and courageous enough to lean under a horse that must have seemed massive in size to her. Most of all, she is brave enough to hold to the belief that we can make it through this when none of the rest of us feel that way.

Reading back what I have written about Trish, I see that perhaps my viewpoint about her is not totally accurate. I based it on what she **USED** to be like. She is not angry all the time anymore (or so she is telling me). I think she is offended by what I wrote. She says she has not called Suzie a 'little creeplet' for a while and has been kinder to her, letting her have the Christmas tree because she likes them. She says she does sometimes go out wearing pink, even though she hates the color. She says she couldn't get everyone out of the ritual setting until she could convince the other four that it was possible to do it and we had somewhere we could hide. She reminds me that she had the escape plan worked out for an Easter years ago, but it was taken forward when the group got their hands on me and made me go through a totally horrendous experience as me/Pat. She admits that yes, if Suzie comes out in public, she gets embarrassed — **BUT** she says she understands what the other four went through better than I do, and she is protecting me from their worst memories until I am in a situation where I don't have to deal with them on my own. As our protector, she says I need outside help to deal with those things.

Oh! And Anne has just said she is sorry, but she feels much more hurt and damaged than I do!

CHAPTER THIRTY-NINE

Forgiveness & Healing Begins

OWNING MY STORY,
AND COMING TO TERMS WITH
MY PAST
WILL BE ONE OF THE BRAVEST
THINGS I HAVE DONE.

DISSOCIATIVE IDENTITY DISORDER DEVON

Quotes Creator

So, it's plain to me that co-consciousness will only happen if we learn to love and care for each other. People have, over the years, taught me how to accept unconditional love. By doing that, it enabled me to learn how to love them in return. Now, I must find ways to love myself. Given the events of the last year, it is not going to be easy. I think self-love suffered a severe setback.

Perhaps I will set that as my first goal in the coming weeks and months: to get back on that journey – to not let the rape take away the progress I made. That would mean he had won twice over! Once I can get back to where I was and keep making progress, I can see myself as someone more deserving of happiness and that I have a purpose other than being abused. Presently, I am too focused on that point. I need to remind myself that **NONE** of the abuse was my fault. I didn't ask for or deserve it. It was caused by people with no sense of morals who enjoyed inflicting pain on whomever they could.

I need to forgive **me**. I don't think I will ever reach the point of forgiving them, but by forgiving myself, I can see myself as a worthy human being who has a purpose beyond victimization. Joyce once said my purpose at this time was running my Dissociative Identity Disorder Devon Facebook page. Now, my mission is that *PLUS* writing this book.

At the beginning of this book, I said I had no idea what would happen when I started writing. I have read it for myself and, as expected, has been full of surprises. It really seems like it has been a joint effort. Things have been written by the others that I knew nothing about. Compared with my previous book,

I hope it has shown more of 'us,' rather than concentrating on the people who have helped me. I think this piece of literary art shows progress in that we are not afraid to talk about us and what we feel.

There are many of us out there fighting the same battles, wondering if there is, indeed, a light at the end of the tunnel. We ask ourselves similar questions:

> Does it ever get better?
> Will we live long enough for it to get better?
> How do we move from "just existing" to living?
> Will the nightmare we are living ever stop?

We **MUST** believe it will improve. Otherwise, there is no point in carrying on.

For me, there is a point to carrying on, even though there are days when I give up and curl up under a fleece with my earphones in. I guess that can serve as self-care, realizing there are days we can't do anything and just need to rest. I have learned that pushing myself beyond my emotional limits backfires on me and makes my mental health worse. I realize, too, that the most critical next step in my recovery is to learn to understand my other personalities and not be so judgmental of them. I need to listen to their stories with compassion and show them compassion. Two years ago, I didn't think I fully understood that. Maybe in my logical brain, I grasped it…but not emotionally. What hasn't changed from my first book to now is my firm belief that **LOVE HEALS.**

Some people believe it is not necessary to hear the trauma of the other personalities. I want to know the stories of others so that I can understand my life in its totality, even if it scares the hell out of me. I know that will be difficult in terms of listening to Cath and Anne. I also acknowledge that to do that, I will need support from professionals. Hopefully, it will one day soon be there. Things are up in the air at the moment with a new care manager on the horizon. Future therapy is not fully decided on. I do, however, honestly believe in what Joyce said to me recently:

"People come into your life at the right time."

I hope the universe is listening because the time is right for the next step!

IN HINDSIGHT...

Earlier, I asked the question, *"Did Pat exist in the first ten days before being adopted?"* I've been thinking about that with considerable depth. In the 1950s, if a mother was giving her child up for adoption, the baby was immediately removed from her after birth. So, for ten days, I would have been in a cot, with the only contact coming from nurses (likely several nurses). Looking back, I think that lack of bonding with my birth mother would have been traumatic for a baby, even though (obviously) I have no recollection of that time. As well, back then, the adoption process was not complete for six months. My birth mother could have changed her mind and wanted me back.

Conversely, my adoptive parents could have also changed their minds and sent me back to an institution to await another set of adoptive parents. How much did that affect any bonding with them if they were unsure as to whether I would stay with them or not? It's likely the first six months of my life were not a good start in terms of bonding, which is so vital for an infant.

I've also been thinking about those with DID who are often told they are "just role-playing." The treatment we receive is very often down to what our therapist, counselor, or psychiatrist thinks or believes. If they don't believe in DID, they tend to think we are just having a mood (for example, acting childish, behaving angrily, or being withdrawn). Others may say, *"If they know they had DID, then they don't have it."* They may 'determine' we are playing different roles deliberately. Every human being plays different roles in their daily life but DID is not role-playing. We do not **CHOOSE** to switch personalities, and we are certainly not faking it.

DID is not caused by a chemical imbalance in my brain. If it were, there would be a medication available — and there isn't. External factors, namely my abusers, caused my DID. What they did to us resulted in my brain not being 'wired' properly. For me, healing involves learning ways of rewiring my brain to determine how it works and reacts. Our mind must learn that we are not constantly under threat of attack, be it emotional, physical, or sexual. Instead, we must learn we are worthy as we are and not worthless as we were always told. We have to learn that what the cult instilled in our mind was not the truth; they were lies. That is much more difficult for some of my personalities than others. It's also important for all of us to learn that our other personalities are not inner demons; rather, they are very damaged parts of me who suffered horrendous abuse. To call them 'demons' links them to the memories of Satanic Ritual Abuse.

The traumas of the last two years (and those of the past) may well be historically in the past, but the flashbacks and nightmares are still there. As well, there are the physical sensations and emotions the incidents created. Therefore, I can't leave them in the past and simply move on with my life. Sometimes, I find myself in a panic and don't know what's causing it. Is it best to distract myself from the panic by using techniques? Or is it best to try and sit with the feelings and figure out what is causing the panic? I suppose a lot depends on whether I am in public or alone. If I am out in public, then I will use a distraction. I can be in social situations where I am easily triggered into the past. For example, being in groups is not only stressful because I switch, but also because being in groups still reminds many of my personalities of being in the ritual group. Because of that, they are always expecting to be abused any minute. Sitting with people in a circle is also triggering for some of them, as it reminds them of ritual settings. Some of my personalities (in particular, Cath and Anne) can't bear to be touched. For them, there is no such thing as 'safe touch.' Even for me, if someone taps me on the shoulder from behind, I will immediately overreact and sense a threat. None of us can cope easily with seeing people in fancy dress or wearing masks. Our mind is instantly transported back into ritual memories.

For many, many reasons, it is difficult for us to live fully in the present. To enjoy the simple things in life is hard when I never know when the next flashback is going to come, when the next switch will happen, and what the consequences of that switch may be. I am so busy trying to look as if I am okay that I find it hard to concentrate on paying attention to the things that are going on around me.

At the end of the day, the solutions lie within 'US.' The right therapist, counselor, or mental health worker can listen and guide. They can teach us techniques and explain to us how trauma has affected us, but all the advice in the world will not help us recover if we are not willing to put in the work ourselves. As everyone with DID is different and our systems work differently, it is up to me to learn about how my system works. To get to know them, I must be willing to listen to them when they want to share with me their stories while showing them the same compassion that Joyce, Sara, and Mary showed me in Scotland. If they could accept and care for me and my others, then surely, it is more important now that I show care and compassion for not only myself but for all my personalities. My P.A. of the last few years accepts and likes whoever she talks to. Maike never judged anyone who spoke to her. In the previous six months, with no consistent mental health worker, it would have been easy to give up. It is then I remind myself that there are many people out there with DID who get no support and somehow manage to keep going. The people who have cared for me over the years and given me support have taught me so much. I can draw on that as I wait to meet my new care manager on January 20, 2020. I need to remind myself that even though my support over the last six months has been sporadic, I can still be willing to build a relationship of trust.

Lastly, since I have started being more open about my history, I have discovered that not everyone will accept or believe my truth. In a way, that is understandable, as some people don't want to accept that such horrendous things can happen to another human being. I suppose it's easier for them to deny what they hear from me. I seldom speak my whole truth (except in books), but I have learned that if I admit to having mental health problems, people will often talk to me about their own issues. On the other hand, some will shy away from me a bit. It's important for me to realize that it is more their problem than it is mine, which is not easy sometimes when mentioning mental health becomes a conversation-stopper.

I met someone recently who read my first book. She admitted she had never heard of DID and found it interesting. She was shocked about the things that happened to me and said she would have never guessed because I always seemed so "normal." I must admit that comment kind of raised a bit of an ironic smile. People with DID do not go around acting like they have two heads or are crazy (thanks, media, for a job well done misconstruing our condition to the unknowing populace). For the most part, we try to hide it and not shout it from the rooftops.

As for "normal," we **ARE** normal. It's what happened to us that wasn't and *never* will be "normal."

Will **I/WE** ever truly heal and recover? I don't know. Perhaps the trauma will never really be healed. I am hopeful that by loving myself and my others, I can lead a fulfilling life where we all live in peace with each other.

ABOUT THE AUTHOR

Pat Suzie Tennent resides in the United Kingdom. Although born in England, most of her life was spent in Scotland where she endured a lifetime of Satanic Ritual Abuse. As a result, her condition—known as Dissociative Identity Disorder—developed as a means to maintain her sanity. In 2015, her journey to recovery from the abuse began when she relocated to England, finally free from the strongholds that kept her bound to her former toxic lifestyle.

Now, at the age of 66, Pat is learning to love both herself and her other personalities. She endeavors to learn how to live in the present while coming to terms with the past. Each day, she makes a valiant effort to look forward to her tomorrows. Pat states, *"Life itself has been my greatest teacher, molding and shaping me into who I am today."*

Pat's sincerest desire is that by writing of her life and sharing the collective stories of her personalities, it will enable others to believe in themselves and to create their own futures.

Pat holds a Bachelor of Theology, Post Graduate Certificate in Pastoral Studies, and a Master of Theology from Aberdeen University. She is also a qualified but not practicing Spiritual Director.

CONNECT WITH PAT SUZIE TENNENT

Follow Pat Suzie Tennent's journey on Facebook
as she works to help others heal and gives them a unique
platform of self-expression:

Dissociative Identity Disorder Devon
www.facebook.com/Dissociativeidentitydisorderdevon

Equine Therapy Associations

United Kingdom:

Sirona Therapeutic Horsemanship
https://sironaequine.org.uk/

United States:

The National Center for Equine Facilitated Therapy
https://www.nceft.org/

*A portion of proceeds from the sales of this book
will be donated to these agencies.*

Pat Suzie Tennent

Printed in Great Britain
by Amazon

37394093R00119